Praise for Clifton L. Taulbert's *When We Were Colored*:

". . . an important, moving work." ANTHONY O. EDMONDS, *Library Journal*

". . . A bittersweet story about love, community and family—and the difference they made in the life of one young man." ROSEMARY L. BRAY, *The New York Times Book Review*

"It depicts an era with a stalwart intimacy that mainstream history books fail to provide." DEBRA TOWNSEND, *San Bernardino Precinct Reporter*

"Above all there emerges from his book warmth and joy, gratitude and affirmation . . ." JOHN KOCH, *The Boston Globe*

"A heartfelt testament to a beleaguered people who maintained dignity and created a viable, caring community . . ." *Kirkus Reviews*

"Well written with good descriptions, it is a gem of a book." BARABARA WEATHERS, *School Library Journal*

"A . . . highly readable . . . tribute to his childhood heroes: a handful of mostly unschooled residents of rural Glen Allen who lifted his sights, made him believe he was special and pointed him toward success . . ." WILLIAM RASPBERRY, *The Washington Post*

PENGUIN BOOKS

THE LAST TRAIN NORTH

Clifton Taulbert, an internationally acclaimed speaker, graduated valedictorian from Greenville, Mississippi's O'Bannon High School, served in a classified position with the 89th Presidential Wing of the United States Air Force, and attended the University of Maine and Maryland. Taulbert received his undergraduate degree from Oral Roberts University, and is a graduate of the Southwest Graduate School of Banking at Southern Methodist University.

He is the President of the Freemount Marketing Company of Tulsa, Oklahoma, where he also serves on numerous civic boards and city trusts. He lives with his wife, Barbara Ann, and their two children, Marshall Danzy and Anne Kathryn.

He is also the author of the award-winning book, *When We Were Colored*.

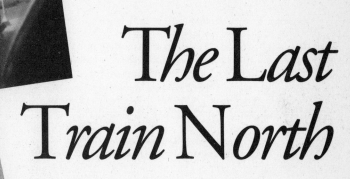

The Last Train North

Clifton L. Taulbert

PENGUIN BOOKS

PENGUIN BOOKS
Published by the Penguin Group
Penguin Books USA Inc., 375 Hudson Street,
New York,New York 10014, U.S.A.
Penguin Books Ltd, 27 Wrights Lane, London W8 5TZ, England
Penguin Books Australia Ltd, Ringwood, Victoria, Australia
Penguin Books Canada Ltd, 10 Alcorn Avenue, Toronto,
Ontario, Canada M4V 3B2
Penguin Books (N.Z.) Ltd, 182–190 Wairau Road,
Auckland 10, New Zealand

Penguin Books Ltd, Registered Offices:
Harmondsworth, Middlesex, England

First published in the United States of America
by Council Oak Books 1992
Published in Penguin Books 1995

1 3 5 7 9 10 8 6 4 2

ISBN 0 14 02.4478 6
(CIP data available)

Printed in the United States of America
Set in Garamond

The Last Train North is the cultural diary of a seventeen-year-old African-American, a native of the Mississippi Delta, who went north during the early 1960s. He was among the last of the migrant dreamers and he went to experience the reality of the dreams he had held all his young life, dreams sparked by the summer visitors from up north, where opportunity abounded and one could sit at the front of the bus. They told of a life of integrated wonder just north of the Mason-Dixon line. . .

The story is dedicated to the significant folks in many of our lives, the parents, grandparents, great-grandparents, aunts, uncles, and all the cousins of the community, who not only packed our lunches of fried chicken and pound cake and placed us in the protective care of the "colored porters," but who also invested their dreams in our generation.

CONTENTS

INTRODUCTION

The Last Train North is not the story of the great migration of African-Americans out of the rural South to the industrialized North. That happened before my time. Our northern relatives had been a part of it, and when they returned to visit us in Glen Allan, Mississippi, they told tales of glory which shaped the character of our dreams. They made those northern cities places of wonder and excitement. This is the story of the last of us who dared to dream about a fully integrated environment and staked our future on the tales told over the years by our annual summer visitors.

The Last Train North begins at the end of an era. The passenger train stopped serving the Mississippi mid-Delta in 1963, a few months after it had carried me north to seek my fortune. When I got to St. Louis the social revolution of the sixties revealed a North of unfulfilled dreams. It wasn't the ideal society of whites and blacks living harmoniously together as had been promised to me by my Aunt Georgia when I was a child.

Aunt Georgia, and other relatives visiting us from up North told us tales of a land of opportunity beyond the segregated South. While standing, hoe in hand, on those long cotton field rows under the spacious Southern skies, my imagination knew no bounds. Whatever I wasn't told, I dreamed. Not deterred by the hot muggy Southern temperatures, I would pick and chop cotton while dreaming of the air-conditioned North. Even the black shiny crows that flew aimlessly overhead seemed to agree with me that the good jobs were up North.

I could hardly wait to go North, and I knew it would be the train, the "high class" mode of transportation, that would make it all reality. Ignoring the sounds of the cotton fields, I spent my days mentally alone, riding the train. That train seemed to me like a grand uncle with a huge cigar, coming to take me North.

But this grand uncle was a neutral party, never letting on that the North of yesteryear was changing. The train just welcomed me aboard and took me to St. Louis, to face the reality of life by myself.

It was an exciting, yet a sad day, when I actually did board the Illinois Central in Greenville, Mississippi, alone and afraid, leaving my family, friends, and community behind. This is the story about what I found there, when I took my last train North, across the Mason-Dixon line.

I have many people to thank for their assistance in the completion of this cultural biography, among them: Jim and Carolyn Hefley and Stephanie Strother of Tulsa; David

Espinoza of Memphis; Loretta Guyton Wilson, Oscar Guyton, Sr., Oscar Guyton, Jr., Dora Brazier, and Arlander Ryan of St. Louis; and my family, Barbara, Marshall, and Anne Kathryn Taulbert; and the editorial department of Council Oak Books, headed by Dr. Sally Dennison.

C. L. T.
MARCH, 1992

The Last Train North

JAMES JENKINS
LEE ANDREW LEWIS

MARGARET JOHNSON
MARY MANNING

FRANK JOHNSON
GENNIE V. M

"A man is limited by his own ambition."

Most Studious--Clifton Talbert and
rgia King realize that continual study
d in attaining their ambition.

CHAPTER ONE

The Last Train North

I t was a major news event. It was covered by Greenville's *Delta Democrat Times*, and all the major Delta radio stations sadly carried the news. It was a day of mourning in Greenville, Mississippi. For almost a century the Illinois Central Railroad had not only carried hundreds of thousands of southern blacks to the cities of the North, but also it had been one of the chief means of transportation for Mississippi Delta whites to travel to and fro. However, the economic considerations of the times and the changing modes of transportation had factored into the decision that caused the old train station to be draped in mourning garb. Today the last engine would puff its way north past Metcalfe into Memphis and eventually to St. Louis, a hub station where all passengers boarded different trains to their final destinations.

On this last day, hoping to be part of history, families were taking short trips. Children were watching as the era that ushered in their parents slowly faded into the distance. Cabs carrying hurried passengers would soon be vying for spots at the bus station instead of the Greenville train depot. Cleaning people who treasured their knowledge of the ins and outs of both the "colored" and "white" waiting rooms at the depot would be without work. The colored porters who loomed larger than life for those of us from the small rural communities would also say goodbye to the Illinois Central — a vehicle that had mobilized the muscles of the South to support the industrialized North.

The train had stopped serving my hometown, Glen Allan, Mississippi, almost twenty years earlier, and only the old folk still talked about those glory days. But Greenville was the Queen City of the Delta and we felt the train would pay homage to her position forever. From the train station located right in the heart of downtown Greenville, this major artery had served its time well. Now one of the South's busiest ports would become a relic, a place to renovate, a sight to point out as one passed walking or driving, a place of poignant memories. Here loved ones left and never returned, but here also had been the focal point of a romantic notion that brought travelling lovers home. Greenville was a queen and the Illinois Central had been a proper suitor, but now the romance was over. The queen was left with only a wooden building bordered by wood and iron rails as a reminder of an affair that had lasted for almost a hundred years.

A few months earlier, I too had been part of this history. I had been among the last residents of Glen Allan to ride the train north out of the Mississippi Delta. Perhaps it was known at the time of my ride that the train would soon stop running, but the news had not yet reached Glen Allan. I boarded the train that day with intentions of riding it over and over again to the South to visit. After all, Ma Ponk, my great aunt who raised me, had said more than once that the better class of people rode the train.

My lifelong ambition had been to view the world from the windows of a train. It was from those small windows that I had hoped to see the lives of fancy people, stately homes and places where whites and blacks worked and played together. And without a doubt in my mind, I knew that the Illinois Central would be the train that would carry me to this place called the North, where I could see for myself the treasures of Cathay, where I, too, could become a modern-day Marco Polo.

As a child of the rural South, I was constantly exposed to

the tales of Northern life from relatives and friends who had moved north, but made their annual pilgrimages south. The factories of the North and East had beckoned many of our families and friends, and I'm told that General Motors even sent buses to the Delta and loaded up laborers. For the most part, however, it had been the train, the Illinois Central that carried the thousands of hopefuls north.

And it had been those hopefuls from the South, the first generations of black migrants, who formed the basis for our dreaming. Armed with strong backs, ambition, dreams, and a little education, they set out to take advantage of the need for labor and better their lives. They went north during the times when the segregated lifestyle of the South was at its height, so that even the limited integration of the North seemed like the promise fulfilled.

Over the years, their stories would keep us dreaming and looking forward to the day when we too would be saying goodbye and boarding the train north. They would laughingly say that even the dirt was different north of the Mason-Dixon line. And we believed all their stories. With each summer, they would return to tell us more. Even though it had happened when I was very young, I recall vividly one special summer visit — that of my Uncle William Henry and Aunt Dora from Chicago. It was one of their annual pilgrimages home. Uncle William Henry, Aunt Dora, and Aunt Georgia had come south to visit their father and brother, my great grandfather, Poppa. And as always, I found myself enthralled with these guests. Uncle William Henry Young had been born in Louisiana, but had come to Glen Allan as a child with Poppa. They had started out as tenant farmers on a place called Ervin in Washington County. But he was not given to field work and as soon as he was able, he headed north to St. Louis. There he had done well, and had soon moved on to Chicago.

We all knew the story. Uncle William Henry had worked hard for American Can and had become an entrepreneur on the side. He and his wife Dora had made a life for themselves. They were members of nearly every church auxilliary and entertained their friends royally. Their home was one of the original Hyde Park mansions and when they visited the South, we saw in them a world of grandeur.

In Glen Allan, they were treated like black royalty. They dressed in suits every day, and their shoes were shined. When they went to the grocery, they would always buy the foods the rest of us could only have on special occasions. Uncle William Henry was tall, stately and smiled with a grin that showed his gold tooth. Aunt Dora was just as captivating with her small dark glasses and well-made suits. When they laughed, we knew they had secrets that only Northerners knew, but we laughed with them, happy for their success and anxiously anticipating our own.

William Henry, Dora and Georgia were Poppa's closest kin, obviously worthy of the best Glen Allan had to offer. In keeping with this position, they were always hosted by Ma Mae.

Ma Mae was another of our seasoned travellers, a native of Mississippi, from the "Hills" down by Fayette by way of Port Gibson and the Delta. I would call her the true Perle Mesta of Glen Allan. And those visits by Uncle William Henry and Aunt Dora always provided her the opportunity to shine. Through her gift of talk and consummate culinary skills, she outwitted all her sisters, which included Ma Ponk, and insured that the Northern guests would make her home their social headquarters.

Although most Southern women were known as good cooks, there were those who managed to bring the mixture of grease and butter to an art form. Ma Mae was such a person. She was Ma Ponk's younger sister and by far the cook of our family. Having gained the reputation for being one of Glen Allan's better cooks as well as a hostess, she had parlayed her culinary skills into a position of prominence. She was a cook to the white community, and it was said she held those white folks hostage through her gastronomical skills. Yet those of us in the "colored" section of Glen Allan were also held captive by the magical mixtures of sugar, butter, and lard that she stirred to perfection. Never mind calories or cholesterol. When the aroma of Ma Mae's food invaded our nostrils, our stomachs had little choice.

Ma Mae was married to Uncle Cleve, the town's ice man, who had bought the old Ballard house and had it redone. Framed by Mississippi cedars and chinaberry trees, the long garret proved to be an inviting place for Northerners to kick back and enjoy the homage being paid them. According to Ma Ponk, Ma Mae would spend her last dime to have a good dinner. No niblets for Ma Mae. Nothing short of a full-course Southern meal would do. This tall Southern lady, carrying with dignity and pride her African, Choctaw, and Jewish genes, would set out to keep her reputation intact. We all knew that Mae would be having dinner for the out-of-town guests. For days she would be sequestered in her kitchen preparing a feast of calories and cholesterol fit for a king. No good Southern meal would be complete without fried chicken, baked sweet potatoes, and the dainty salads that Ma Mae would make. The smells from her oven, especially the aroma from her famous lemon pound cake, would fill the street by her house.

Humming as she worked, Ma Mae cooked and cleaned with a passion. Her rooms were immaculate, including the guest room. Most black families in Glen Allan were lucky to have a separate bedroom, but Ma Mae always had a guest room that seemed like an oasis in the desert. Her guest room almost rivaled her cooking. Though small, it was definitely not a room to use every day. It was more like a fantasy world, where, after a hard day's work in the field or in the kitchen, one could open the door and escape to a place of beauty, if only for a few minutes.

Covered with a thick and expensive pink chenille spread, the bed with its tall oak posts occupied the vast majority of the floor space. Pink organza ruffled curtains, crisscrossed to add fullness, cast a pink spell over the room. On rare occasions, with permission, I would be allowed to go into this sanctuary to get guest towels from the matching chest of drawers. While careful not to track mud on her shiny linoleum, I was always fascinated by the tall victrola and the dresser that held bottles of unused perfume. In this room, so different from the rest, Ma Mae would also store her winter canned food as well as her prized quilts that were used for company. Her bed, plump and feathered, was always a delight to secretly jump upon knowing that one day, I too would be a visitor and Ma Mae would let me sleep in the room that, for now, I could only dream about.

Ma Mae made the North real. For when the northern relatives came South, she became part of the story that validated their claim to the good life. From her use of the good china and her mayonnaise dressing, Ma Mae created a reception that stayed firmly impressed upon my mind. For years, I would watch her children, Mamie and Uncle Leroy as well as

Ginnie Lee, Nootsey, and others come home to be treated like kings and queens. Feted to the best of her cooking skills and allowed to slide between the starched sheets that were reserved for guests, they made life north of the Mason-Dixon line look great. And I could hardly wait until it was my turn to go north and return triumphantly to the South of my birth. It would be years before I would be feted to a full-scale dinner prepared by Aunt Willie Mae, but the wait would be worth it. And I would eventually get my chance to slide between the starched guest sheets.

But this summer, I was still a boy, and it was Aunt Dora, Aunt Georgia, and Uncle William Henry who received the honors. As usual, they dined with Ma Mae and went around the lake to see old friends. Poppa enjoyed them, and I was impressed. Now their annual visit was over; the dream-makers were returning north. They were packed and ready to return to Chicago.

I was sitting on Poppa's tall steps, looking and admiring these people who yearly would come in and out of our lives. I was quiet, just sitting on the steps, when the old screen door opened, and they came tumbling out of the front room with all their suitcases. Now smiles turned to tears and the handshakes to hugs. There was nothing anyone could do to keep them in Glen Allan.

There were goodbyes and promises of more frequent

visits. Too young to be part of the parting, I just sat and looked into their faces as they slowly brushed past me down the long steps to my uncle's waiting car. Aunt Georgia, Poppa's sister, was always the last to leave. Just before she kissed Poppa goodbye, she reached down and patted me on the head.

"You wanna come North and live with me?" she said. "It's not like it is here. My boys play with the white boys who live next door. They eat at each other's house. Your mama will let you come."

Of course, I was too young to leave at the moment, but I could hardly wait my turn. Visions of large brick homes, a world of integration, suits worn every day, and joyful visits back home became a real part of my life. From then on, I began to look beyond the South, and to prepare myself for life in St. Louis, Chicago, or Detroit.

And many days when there was little else to do I would sit and daydream. I could imagine myself dressed in a double-breasted suit like Cousin Earl or wearing a stingy-brimmed hat like Uncle Leroy's with small dark glasses and my hair neatly pressed to my head. I could imagine myself being met at the train station in Greenville. I could hardly wait.

The train station was a grand world to us, and everyone was dressed up, even those coming to meet their guests. We didn't give much thought to the separate "colored" and "white" waiting rooms, but we bathed in the smell of the fumes and the sound of the engine that carried our hopes north and brought home the tales of their discovery. I knew that the train would be there for me, puffing and waiting with the delightful colored porters ready to assist me and announce my return home.

And they would all be there to meet me, Poppa, Mary my mother, Ma Ponk and Aunt Willie Mae. Those would be good days. Taking the train north and returning home to the delight of family and friends was the fantasy that would hold my attention for years as I attended school, worked in the fields, and dreamed of life north of the Mason-Dixon line.

The summer visits of relatives and friends would come and go but I would stay behind with Mama and Poppa, and I would receive other invitations, but I would always remember the day Aunt Georgia described the North and a world of integration that would shape my expectations.

There were more summers of chopping cotton, working at the post office, raking fig leaves for Mrs. Knight, and working as a utility man at the Hilton's Food Store. While at Hilton's working, I would often talk with Ray Quong, the son of T.Y., the Chinese grocer whose store was next door to Hilton's. After sweeping the sidewalk clean and washing the windows, I would sit and talk with Ray about which of us would be the first to leave Glen Allan. It made for good conversation while we both waited for the Saturday night grocery crowd.

I especially loved those old black people who would come into town on Saturday night with their hard-earned money, social security checks to be cashed and their barely legible list of groceries to be filled. They all knew my folks, especially Poppa. I was expected to be polite and mannerly, and I was.

Many times they'd come on the back of borrowed trucks or catch a ride with friends and relatives. Dressed modestly with hats and purses, the men in starched khaki pants and shirts, they brought excitement to the store. Feeling like the king of the meat cutters, I could hardly wait to fill their orders of center-cut pork chops, neck bones, and chickens. I was always careful to say "yesum" and "nossir" as well as "thank you" and "come again." It made them feel good having me there to fill their orders, sack their groceries, and take the sacks out to the trucks for them. But they all knew that one day I'd be leaving Hilton's going north. They would wish me the best, somewhat saddened, but understanding.

Finally in May of 1963, I graduated from O'Bannon High School in Greenville, Mississippi, as the Valedictorian of my class. After years of standing on the long cotton rows watching out for the visitors to come home again and tell their tales, I was ready to go north myself. Glen Allan could not make my dreams come true, and I was determined to see them become a reality north of the line.

Shortly after my graduation, I received a letter and a one-way train ticket on the Illinois Central to St. Louis. The letter and ticket had come from a man I'd never met — my father. He'd left the South before my birth and now lived in St. Louis where he was a Baptist preacher. Now that I was grown and wanting to seek my fortune in the North, he had been called upon to help me make the transition. He had arranged for me to stay with some very close friends of his, people who, though not related to him by blood or marriage, were his extended family with ties that went back to his own Mississippi childhood. They owned a grocery store and I had grocery store experience. Although I had never seen them before, they agreed to welcome me to their St. Louis home.

And so it was that, in 1963, I said goodbye to the Mississippi Delta and to the community that had given me life. Armed with great expectations and visions of a promised world of northern grandeur, I boarded the train north.

As that train left the Mississippi Delta, I didn't know that I would witness the ending of an era, that the "North" in my mind, created by the Southerners who had been part of the great migrations, was disappearing, and in its stead was a reality of growing discontent among urban blacks.

Though I would be enchanted by the grandeur of the St. Louis train station, the hundreds of trains and the thousands of people, I was somewhat unprepared for the reality of my northern existence, living in a small room over a neighborhood grocery store.

To be certain, the well-dressed summer visitors had found for themselves a bit of equality north of the Mason-Dixon line. So rigid were the rules of their former segregated South that they cherished the light of integration coming from the slightly-ajar northern door. They translated this glimmer of hope into marvelous tales of a wonderful life.

Though opportunities to earn higher wages characterized the North, and that was part of my motivation for that last train ride, I could never forget the quest for an education that had been part of my southern rearing. More than anything, I wanted to go to college and earn a degree. In St. Louis I searched for jobs that would afford me the opportunity to go to school, as opposed to those "colored" jobs that held only the promise of retirement.

The Civil Rights movement of the sixties would come alive for me in my northern city, St. Louis. The disparity between the oft-told summer tales and the reality of urban living would collide on the streets, and there I would watch as the third and fourth generation blacks with southern roots took to the streets and dispelled the myth of the treasures of Marco Polo. I had come north at the end of the last chapter and the beginning of a new book.

The North of the 1960's was being reshaped not only by the urban social upheaval, but also by a war that was claiming her sons in an unprecedented number. Vietnam was rewriting history and my personal history would not be excluded.

Still determined to be a Northerner, I quickly picked up new and improved dressing habits while learning to speak with a distinct Northern ring. However, my process of becoming Northern would be interrupted by the military as I took another train ride, to Texas and boot camp.

But on that Saturday afternoon in 1963, filled with hope, fear and anticipation as I boarded the last train north from the Delta, I hardly envisioned my dreams being interrupted by war, riots, and racism. I would soon be facing a new reality, and the wisdom of those who had nurtured me would become increasingly more important. Poppa, Ma Ponk, Mr. Fields, Mother Luella Byrd, Mama, and the others became the strength that held my dreams together. Though death invaded their ranks, they remained very much alive and nurturing in my memory. And when the prospect of a Vietnam assignment became overwhelming, these memories of the Delta and my silent heroes became the stories that eased my fears. They were the people that I would later write about, those wonderful colored people, the ones who had seen me off when I took the last train north.

CHAPTER TWO

Pullman Porters, Ma Mae's Chicken, and St. Louis

F ear and excitement kept me occupied that summer afternoon in 1963 as I nestled down in the colored section of the train. My young mind was filled with wonder as the big train pulled out of Greenville heading north. Even though St. Louis was my destination, Metcalfe, Memphis, and all the points in between were just as exciting. Remembering Ma Ponk's instructions, I kept my eyes focused on the colored porter. I watched as he confidently walked the

aisles, handing out pillows, and frequently checking his gold pocket watch.

As the porter got closer to my seat his face broke out in a big grin. Reaching out and patting me on the head, he said, "First time huh?"

"Yes sir," I answered, trying to look and act grown up. But the porter was a pro and he could always spot the first time riders. Glancing around the coach, I tried to find a familiar face from Glen Allan, but none were to be found, just well-dressed strangers, their eyes filled with hope, heading north.

As we rode north I could occasionally overhear a conversation from one or two of the riders. They all seemed excited, glad to be going north to see their dreams come true. I caught only bits of their conversation, but I heard them speak in wonder about the life awaiting them. I knew it must be a good life because so many people had left before them. Now I was joining the migration. Dressed in my casual best and holding my packed supper securely by my side, I nervously glanced out the small windows as the old train puffed its way through Metcalfe.

I had been to Metcalfe a few times before, but it looked different out of a small train window. It seemed at times that the train was standing still and I was watching the pecan trees and shotgun houses run past my window. Sometimes I'd see a few children standing in their small yards waving and waving when we passed each other. Then, Metcalfe became a distant blur, and as it faded from my sight I began to feel the impact of what was happening. Today I was leaving home for good. This was not a short ride to Jackson with my Uncle Cleve. I was leaving Poppa's house where I was born, leaving Ma Ponk's house which I had called home for nearly twelve years. I was leaving my security—the familiar gravel streets of Glen Allan's colored section. But as I traveled, the people who had loved me and encouraged me to stay in school and study hard were all crowded into my mind. They had also packed their bags and headed north with me. The fields, the houses, the churches, and even the old field trucks were left behind, but the people, my community, they too had gotten aboard the train when the conductor called out, "Last call! All aboard."

I sat for a long time, fighting tears and watching Washington County, Mississippi slowly fade into the long rows of cotton waiting to be chopped. Finally I settled back into the seat. Still somewhat unsure of what my limitations were, I tried to keep from having to use the bathroom. Somewhere north of Metcalfe, however, nature won out. The colored porter became my guide, assuring me that the small room at the end of the train was capable of handling my needs.

Whether I should leave my supper bag on the seat or take it with me now became a monumental question. I remembered Ma Ponk's advice to watch out for thieves. But, finally, leaving the sack on the seat won out, and I walked down the aisle to the rest room. I felt as if every eye in the coach was upon me. But I looked straight ahead and within a short span of time I had successfully used the bathroom. The aisle back seemed strangely long, and panic began to set in. My face must have expressed my fear because the old porter smiled and gently pointed to the empty seat two rows up from him.

For decades, the colored porters had served as ambassadors for colored folks who rode the train. They made sure that we understood the rules and that we safely reached our destinations. Due to their care in guiding us through the Jim Crow South, hundreds of thousands of blacks arrived unharmed.

We didn't know the porters' names. Most of them were simply called "George." Whatever the day or time, any one of the porters would answer when he heard a call for "George." The porters had names, families, and dreams, but it was a different time then. They went dutifully about their jobs answering to "George" and making life easier for thousands of railroad passengers. Though trained to serve during an era that minimized their human equality while maximizing their service skills, they were a proud cadre of professionals. Now it was my turn to be guided safely north by a kind and skillful black porter.

The seat was mine, my sack was on it, and here was my

own window. We were all together now. I eased into the comfort of the train and let the monotonous sound of the engine keep me awake as I tried to picture the transformation that would take place the moment the train crossed the Mason-Dixon line.

As I hunkered down in my seat, I thought about the future. Not only was I heading north for the first time in my life, but at the end of this train ride I would be met by a complete stranger— my father.

I had never seen this man, only heard his voice once, a few weeks before, on the telephone. Until then, I had barely even known of his existence. When I was little I always assumed the man my mama was married to was my father. I was the oldest of six children, and even though we all lived in Glen Allan, I was the only one of the family who didn't live with Mama and Dad. I had never thought much about why I had been singled out for the honor of living with my great grandfather, Poppa, and later with my great aunt Ma Ponk. I just assumed it had something to do with my being oldest, the automatic heir to special privileges.

I could remember several instances from my early childhood when some of the older people would look at me and say, "he sho' looks like . . ." But as I approached them, their conversations would trail off. They would look at me and smile, but I was never told what they were talking about. Later

I knew that I had been born before my mother and father were married, but I didn't realize there might be more to it than that. I knew who my mother was, and who my father was — I thought.

However, several years after Mama was divorced from my stepfather — the only father I knew — I learned that those long-ago silenced conversations were true. My father was the stranger people talked about, but I never knew. While Mama was just a young girl she had become involved with the handsome young Mississippi riverboat gambler turned preacher. Willie Jones from Davis Bend, Mississippi, was indeed my father.

My great-grandparents had wrapped their love around my mother and provided me a place to call home and a family to call mine. It was their love, so real and warm, that kept me from becoming overly concerned about those silenced conversations. Momma Pearl and Poppa knew that regardless who my father really was, they were without question my great-grandparents and my mother was their little girl. With little education themselves, they wanted the best for her, so they said, "Until you get through school and get married, we'll raise the boy." And even after Mama married, they continued to love me and provide a safe place for the baby that had been born unexpectedly.

Then, after my high school graduation, it was explained

to me that my "real" father was a prominent black community leader in St. Louis, a Baptist pastor who was the president of a Bible training center. He had arranged for me to fulfill my lifelong dream, to move north. I was to live with close friends of his in St. Louis, help out around their grocery store, and find work.

On the phone my father's voice had sounded warm and welcoming as he talked about plans for my relocation to St. Louis, but now I wondered what he would be like when I saw him face to face. How would he treat me? And what would he think of me?

The anticipation of meeting for the first time the man who had given me life was more than my young mind could bear, so I turned my thoughts to other things. I tried to picture St. Louis. I knew it was big, because so many people had described the size. I had not seen pictures, but I had seen visitors from there. They were St. Louis to me, all dressed up in their suits, dark glasses, and driving shiny cars. They conjured up a world of beauty and equality that I could not imagine. I thought of Lucille, Mama's cousin who always sent boxes of clothes, and also Mama's good friends Cager and Ellen Ruth Maxey. They would come down to our house to see Mama. I remember Ellen as being very light-skinned with long hair. She had always been very nice to me and Mama. Like many northern visitors, Ellen called Mama "Mary Ester," her complete name, which was hardly ever used in Glen Allan. Then there was Jake who would also come home and of course Glen Allan would be all abuzz. Jake owned a tavern in St. Louis. I also thought about Memphis, just up the road, and the crossing of the Mason-Dixon line.

Unlike the bus, which stopped at every turn, the train only stopped at major train stations. Of course Ma Ponk had told me all about the train and how it was the better ride.

"Yes sir," she had often said, "the bus stops for everybody whether they can breathe or not. A better class of people rides the train." Ma Ponk had never forgotten her first—and last—bus ride. After that ride, she swore before Jesus that lack of money and death would be the only reasons she'd ever again pile herself in the back of anybody's bus.

Ma Ponk's trips uptown to Glen Allan to get her mail would often bring out her disdain for riding the bus. The Glen Allan post office was next to the drugstore, which also doubled as the bus stop. Right in front of the drug store's big picture window was the yellow bench where the whites sat — and the blacks stood — waiting for the bus.

"Look at 'em lined up like flies, piling on the bus," Ma Ponk would say. "You can't even get in Miss Margit's store. Look there's Lulu Harris from the colony. She got good money, but she gonna get on that bus."

Ponk muttered her distaste for the bus, but she'd always

quit muttering in time to smile and speak to the likes of cousin Lulu from the colony. Then, when she completed her task of getting the mail, we'd head to the back of Glen Allan, but not before she'd made one last comment for the road.

"It's gonna take 'em nearly two days to get where they's going. Dat bus is gonna stop at ever Tom, Dick and Harry's."

Of course she was right. Just the summer before my mother and I had taken a bus ride to Memphis, and true to form, the bus did stop at every store, and sometimes at railroad crossings. At the time it was exciting to me to watch all the different people getting on, crowding into the bus. Many of them had been making one-way trips north. For Mama and me, it was a round trip. We would visit a cousin and an outdoor tent service, and then we'd return home to Glen Allan.

And so I sat quietly in my train seat, grateful not to be riding the bus. I watched the daylight being left behind as the train sped past little plantation towns that were major bus stops.

At last, I found myself getting hungry. By now, the brown bag that held my supper was greasing from the inside out. The grease from Ma Mae's fried chicken and Miss Callie's homemade butter had made the brown bag almost translucent. I could smell and almost see straight through to that home-cooked meal. I wasn't quite sure about the proper time to eat, but I decided to go ahead.

Sitting there alone on the train surrounded by strangers going to an exciting new world, I felt that brown-bag supper was more than a hold-over from the world I was leaving behind. It was love, wrapped in tastes and smells. And for those few minutes while I silently ate, trying not to get crumbs on my pants, I was not alone. The fried chicken and pound cake from that brown bag took me back to the big dining room at Poppa's house where Ma Mae and Ma Pearl had shared the common kitchen.

Sundays, when all the field work was over, we'd be feted to big family Sunday dinners. Ma Mae was the queen of the Sunday dinner in Glen Allan. She ruled whatever kitchen she entered as her rightful domain. Tall, light skinned, and slightly overweight, she would hum to herself as she prepared the magical feast. And the old black four-eyed iron stove with the warmer at the top did her bidding, always cooking the food to perfection.

Ma Mae had insisted on making my supper for this, my epocal journey north. Ma Ponk, her sister, had agreed, and had packed the food in this brown bag, sending with it her love. I felt surrounded by that love as I finished my little meal. It was now official: Glen Allan had sent yet another son north.

No one else on the train seemed to be concerned with me. The porter was busy now getting ready to pull into Memphis.

I turned my thoughts back to my dreams of the future. Had it not been for the occasional sight of the shotgun houses lining the end of the fields, my dreaming would have had me long since out of Mississippi. But the Illinois Central kept passing by reminders that looked so much like home.

Chinaberry trees, pecan trees and a few southern pines went by my window, and as I watched them, I became sleepy. With little else to do, I reached down and made sure that my money was still tucked inside my socks. Ma Ponk had told me to hide my money because thieves were always looking for an easy mark. Secure that my money was safe and my stomach full, I nestled in the corner of my seat and fell asleep, but I determined not to sleep through Memphis and the crossing of the Mason-Dixon line.

I was soon awakened by the sound of the porter talking to an old black man who was sitting a couple of seats ahead of me.

"We'll be in Memphis shortly. The train's making good time now. Don't you fret, I'll make sure you git to where your daughter can see you and git you picked up."

"Memphis," I thought to myself. I had never seen the Memphis train station. Ma Ponk and Ma Mae said it was big, yes, much bigger than the one in Greenville; but it was nothing compared to the one in St. Louis. They told me the St. Louis train station was about as big as all of Glen Allan. I had never seen any buildings that big, nor had I ever been to a major northern city. I could hardly wait. All my years had been preparing me for this moment. Every northern visitor had told virtually the same tale about the integrated life that happened just north of the Mason-Dixon line. I couldn't wait to cross that line. I wanted to see the North and feel her welcome. This, my first train ride, would see me enter that reality . . .

"Wake up boy, we' at St. Louis." The colored porter was shaking me. "I said wake up. It's time for you to get off."

I awoke with a start. Apparently, I had been very tired, because I had slept right through Memphis and all the little towns that I really wanted to see. Worst of all, I had missed seeing the Mason-Dixon line. I had wanted so badly to see the place where segregation ended and integration began. But as I sleepily peered out the small window, I saw a world of wonder. Hundreds, maybe thousands of people of all races were huddled together, walking back and forth as the huge trains pulled into their designated slots and started loading and unloading passengers. I might have stared forever had it not been for the kindly porter. Responding to his grandfatherly prodding, I managed to get my small bag and walk down the aisle with him.

As we both walked off the train, I became even more amazed. Now I was able to see the full size and grandeur of the train station. It was so tall, with huge window panes in the ceiling to allow the rays of sun to dance upon the polished marble floors. There were rows and rows of long brown benches, highly polished, holding people who were dressed equally as well. As the vastness of the station and the number of the people began to overwhelm me, I remembered Aunt Willie Mae's advice.

"St. Louis is a big city and the train station is 'bout as big as Glen Allan," she had said. "Course the first time I went north, I almost got lost in that station. But I was determined to find my folks or let them find me. Honey, I got off the train and there ain't a soul there. Now, we's always careful about time in the South, but up there, they sorta move a little different. So I just waited on one of them long benches. You'll see 'em the minute you git off the train. The place's too big for you to go rambling 'round, so you just plant yourself in one spot and don't move. They'll find you. Yes sir, they'll find you. It's better them lost than you."

With such sage advice from a seasoned traveler, I located me a safe spot not too close to the tracks, and I just stood there, looking at every searching face, trying to find a pair of eyes that would connect and light up when seeing me. I hadn't told the porter I was being met by my father — only that "someone" was meeting me. I didn't know how to explain that I didn't know the man and he didn't know me. As I stood there, fully aware that the comfort of Glen Allan was behind me, I felt fear and excitement at the same time. I watched scores of "colored" porters scurrying with racks loaded with matching luggage, followed by families all secure in the fact that they were in the right place. I didn't know if I was in the right place or not. I just stood there. Somehow I knew that someone would come to get me. As I watched and waited, the old porter who had safely guided me from Greenville to St. Louis came over and gave me a last comforting hand shake and assured me that my folks would be there soon to take me home.

And the porter was right.

"Well, it's Clifton," a voice said. I turned to see a tall, well-dressed colored stranger. He was holding my high school graduation picture.

"Yes sir," I replied. As I nervously shook his hand I realized that I was meeting a little bit of myself: the stranger with my picture must be my natural father. He was a tall greying man in his fifties. He had a small mustache and was well dressed in a grey suit. In his hand, along with my picture, he held a black straw hat. We picked up my one suitcase.

Ma Ponk had securely locked the suitcase and then strapped it with an extra leather belt. According to her, you didn't want to trust the locks because with all the handling, a person could lose all his belongings. Ma Ponk had done a good job as always. The suitcase had arrived intact.

I was too excited and scared to talk. I just looked and looked as my father and I made our way out of the large train station. I was amazed to see a huge water fountain monument of mythological sea beings spewing water high into the St. Louis sky. This was the city; there was no doubt in my mind. The streets were all paved, and the colored people were all dressed up, and the buildings were incredibly tall. As I stared at the wonders of my new surroundings, my mind raced back and forth between St. Louis and Glen Allan, comparing the people, measuring the length, width and the height of the buildings. There was no smell of cotton in St. Louis. There were no shotgun houses, no muddy streets. Here I saw hundreds of shiny cars—Cadillacs included—moving constantly up and down the broad street. For sure we were in the North. Even though I'd been asleep, we had crossed the Mason-Dixon line.

I was almost breathless as I viewed this new world. I became even more confident that the Marco Polo tales of Cathay were true when my father ushered me into a black Cadillac. I tried not to show my absolute childish excitement, but riding in this car was a dream come true. I didn't know where the man was taking me or where I would stay, but I felt confident that this stranger and his car would find the place I would eventually call home.

As we sped past the tall buildings of St. Louis, I sat quietly on the passenger's side and tried to answer my father's questions about the people back home. Some of them I knew, but others I only knew by their names. He smiled as we talked, and I looked with disbelief as he pointed out huge colored churches that were bigger than the white Methodist church I had helped to clean in Glen Allan. He seemed to enjoy talking about the old folk he had known as a boy growing up in the Delta, but a note of pride entered his voice as he showed me St. Louis. We passed some skyscrapers that he called projects, and streets with names like Laclede and Grand. St. Louis was big, exciting, and scary.

As the car swiftly moved through the St. Louis streets, the conversation slowed down. I was north, I thought. I had told my childhood acquaintance Ray Quong that one day I would leave. Now, here I was in St. Louis, the city of all my dreams.

But I began to feel sad as I thought about those familiar Saturday nights in Glen Allan when all the plantation people would come to town to get their week's supply of groceries. As my newfound father talked and pointed out buildings and sites of interest, I realized that those Saturday nights at Hilton's were gone for good. Miss Bea, Cousin Lulu, the folks from Grace, Valewood, and PanterBurn would soon become to me like his memories were to him—life from a distant past that never quite moved north, but would always travel with us.

"Well, boy, we'll be there in twenty-five minutes," my

father said. "They can't wait to see you."

His minutes were like years as I tried to figure out the "they." Who were they? How would they look? How big would their house be? Would I have my own bedroom? Would Miss Beulah be nice like Ma Ponk? And as we talked about them, I tried to picture them in my mind.

According to my father, the people I was going to live with were relatives of his who owned their own grocery store. I pictured tall men dressed in striped suits like Uncle William Henry, with slicked-back hair and gold teeth prominently spaced. For all those hot southern summers, I had seen those northern colored gentlemen and also the ladies, with their faces magnificently painted, always wearing little dark glasses and brightly colored pants. I was north now and I couldn't wait to meet my new family and see the place I would soon call home.

CHAPTER THREE

The Confectionery: Mr. Madison's Place

My mind was bursting with fear and excitement as I rode in the Cadillac down Market Street framed by Gothic buildings from another era. Occasionally my father and I talked as he drove, but most of the way we just sat and I watched the city unfold in front of my eyes. From Market Street we took a turn onto Franklin Street where I saw more colored people than ever. They were going in and out of stores, carrying bags of food. Many just stood on the corners. While slowly driving down Franklin, I saw an endless number of one-way soul food restaurants that specialized in the foods of the South, from chitterlings to collard greens with candied sweet potatoes. And there were plenty of beauty parlors where ladies could get their hair pressed, curled and styled, and even weaved if necessary.

According to my newly-acquired chauffeur and father, Franklin Street was really Mississippi and Alabama all on one street. He laughingly said, "If you ever want to find yo' kin, just stand on the corner of Franklin and yell their name. Somebody will know them." And I would later learn that he was right. Not only in St. Louis, but in every major northern city, there was one street that seemed dedicated to reminders of home.

We laughed our way from Franklin to Grand, where we crossed such high-class-sounding streets as Laclede and Cote Brilliante. Still impressed with the grandeur of Union Station and the frenzy on Franklin, I now marvelled at the Koontz Funeral Home building and the huge "colored" churches that we passed. As we sped down Grand Avenue, my father proudly pointed out the famous Busch Stadium, the home of the St. Louis Cardinals. Even in Glen Allan, we knew about the Cardinals and what I didn't know I would soon learn from cousin Pearl, a native of Glen Allan who lived within walking distance of the St. Louis stadium. Cousin Pearl was Cousin Savanah's sister and she had been among the family visitors who kept our dreams alive. Soon, of course, I would visit her and get to know other relatives who now called St. Louis home.

Eventually, we exited off Grand onto St. Louis Avenue (such big sounding names!) where I saw double row brick houses that were occupied by black people. As we drove down St. Louis Avenue to Spring, we passed rows and rows of houses closely packed together with periodic patches of green. We kept driving. I saw little children playing in their yards and occasionally running into the streets to retrieve their balls. They all seemed happy. They were Northerners, blessed with street lights, paved sidewalks, and houses that had quarters upstairs. However, as we continued our drive, I saw no white faces. I felt certain I would soon see them and their houses, however. After all, I was now in the integrated North.

I was so immersed in watching the passing scenes, I hardly noticed when the car slowed down.

"Well boy, here we are at your new address, 2629 North Spring Avenue," said my father. "Com'on, let's get your bag and go in and meet the folk."

As I made my way out of the nice shiny car, I was somewhat taken aback. I had been so busy admiring the cathedrals and public buildings that I had somehow not noticed a consistent change which had taken place as we drove further and further from the grandeur of the downtown train station. Suddenly I realized I was not in the northern neighborhood of my dreams. I no longer saw grandeur. There were no long porches with well-dressed men and ladies lounging about. All I saw was a two-story brick building discolored by decades of soot. The place had a screen door and bars on the windows. There was no lawn, just a few weeds that were trying to break their way through the cracks in the sidewalk.

Was this the place which I'd been told I would live, the single building which housed a grocery store at the street level and living quarters above? Surely this was a mistake. This building was way too small. I desperately looked for numbers over the door, but I could barely make them out beneath the layers of dirty paint.

It was the place. My father nodded in the direction of that corner building and told me happily, "Just across the street, boy. Yeah, that Madison's place. He and Dora has done well up here. I knew Dora's mama back in Mississippi. Good people. They gonna treat you right."

He pushed a button inside his car which caused the back trunk to open. So unlike Poppa's car or any of the others I had seen in Glen Allan, the Cadillac was keeping alive my dream of what living in the North was all about. But as I pulled from the trunk my suitcase which was strapped with Ma Ponk's old belt, I noticed that this one piece of luggage which had seemed so out of place in the large downtown train station, seemed quite at home on North Spring.

"Come on. Let's meet the folk," said my father. I walked slowly behind as he led me across the street. Suddenly I realized that today, more than the night when I graduated, I was a man, on my own. Food, rent, and clothing were going to be my responsibility from now on. Glen Allan had sent a child north and they would expect a northern man to return. No time for tears or reconsideration. Between me, the curb and the side-walk was my future, Madison's place, properly called Brazier's Confectionery. It was not quite the grocery store I had envisioned, nor the street I had dreamed about. The city smell of perfume and cologne did not fill the air, only exhaust fumes from the steady stream of vehicles that prodded their way on this much-traveled street.

My reflections were interrupted by children yelling and dogs barking as they dashed out the screen door of the store. I now saw faces peering through the barred windows and eyes trying to focus on me. I was expected. But was I what they expected? It was such a short distance from the car to the store, but the walk seemed to take forever.

I observed the small neighborhood that Madison's place anchored. The houses were all two-story, mostly brick, though a few were frame. Each house seemed to have its own patch of greenery. But the store was on the corner and the only greenery I saw were the small weeds that were trying to break their way through the holes in the concrete sidewalk. The store, small from outside appearances, was somewhat similar to the little corner stores I had seen in the Delta.

Then my father swung open the screen door and we walked into the dimly lit store. The place was crowded with old people and vegetable boxes. Hands now extended toward me and faces smiled at me and all my new St. Louis relatives began to talk at once, welcoming me to the North.

"Let me look at you boy!"

"Yeah, they sho' fed you well."

"He's from the South, still says yes'em and nossir." That was from the matriarch, Mama Beulah, a short, bright-skinned lady with brown hair, lipstick, rouge, and painted finger nails. She was born in the South, but had come to St. Louis as a young woman. She looked and dressed the northerner's part. Her speech was sharp and pointed, not quite warm and endearing, but pleasant just the same. They all deferred to her as she began to question me and trace my family tree. I would later learn that "tree tracing" was not an uncommon northern event. It seems as if the northern folks wanted to be assured that a newcomer had good southern roots, some of which they knew.

As Mama Beulah climbed my family tree she must have been pleased with the fruit she picked because she finally said, "Put your grip down, you' at home now." The store, and maybe even St. Louis, sighed with relief as she gave her approval.

"I want you to meet Brother," she said as she personally guided me behind the old meat counter to a tall big black man, totally bald, with the whitest teeth I had ever seen. Brother — Mr. Brazier, that is — was her son-in-law. Mr. Madison Brazier in his own way had made his northern dream come true. The landlord of tenement houses, the proprietor of his own grocery store, he was considered a capitalist—a man with money. He verbally ruled, but I'm convinced that Mama Beulah pulled the strings, using her pretty light-skinned daughter Dora as her key.

From Mr. Madison to Aunt Clara who ran the store to the store regulars, I guess I must have shaken at least a dozen hands. There wasn't much room to move around, and I anxiously looked to see which door would lead to the grand living quarters upstairs. My father, somewhat assured of my acceptance, took me aside for a private conversation. Quietly he explained that he had a family, even though he cared deeply about me. He said he was an orphan, with no knowledge of his own father, and he understood how I must feel. Still, we would probably never be able to have the father-son relationship that we both wanted. Madam, as he called his wife, would prefer that I remained a closed chapter in their lives.

I guess I understood. I was north and his folks at the confectionery seemed like nice people. But suddenly I felt more alone than ever before as I realized something I hadn't quite understood before. Even though he had met me at the train and promised to introduce me to all my relatives, my father's invitation to me had been to come north, not to come home. My father purchased himself a large Vess soda and bid me farewell. After a few more handshakes and questions from around the confectionery about my family tree, I was taken upstairs to where I would live. The stairs excited me, because in Glen Allan, only white peoples' homes were two stories tall. Now here I was being taken upstairs to my room. The creak of the stairs, the musky smell, the dim lights didn't bother me at all. I had to walk quickly to keep up as I followed Mama Beulah — the lady who wielded the power of Spring Street.

Because of how Mama Ponk had described her son's home in Highland Park, I believed that the end of the stairs would expand into a glorious house filled with rooms and light. I could hardly wait. But not so. As we made our way to the top of the stairs Mama Beulah said matter-of-factly, "You gonna share this middle room with Michael." I peered through the door into a crowded little room. Where was the bed? I looked, but I couldn't find one. And who would this Michael be?

Mama Beulah kept moving. My eyes followed her short body as she confidently and proudly strutted through an archway that led to a room that looked onto the main street. "This big front room with the window is mine," she said.

By now I had dropped my bag on the floor and was trailing the leader. She stuck her head out of the bedroom door and pointed down the narrow hall.

"The back bedroom belongs to Clara and Sam, and the bathroom's right here, across the hall, right down from the kitchen. It's a nice place. Consider yourself real lucky. When I first come north I boarded with the roaches."

I finally discovered the hideaway bed in my little room and pulled it out. There were no chairs. I sat on the small bed, slightly bigger than the cot I had left in Glen Allan. I wanted to cry, but I didn't. I just sat there for a moment trying to decide on whether or not I should go to the restroom. I really needed to answer nature's call, but I wanted to wait until Mama Beulah had gone back downstairs. So much had happened so quickly, but not all of it like I had dreamed.

The restroom was not that difficult to find. It was right across the hall, and the hall was extremely narrow. I found it and it worked. After washing up, I went back to the middle room where I again sat on the pulled-out bed and began to think. While thinking, I quietly and soberly observed my new surroundings. The brightly colored wall paper, surrounded by a chest of drawers and partially opened boxes, seemed to crowd in at me as I tried to relax. The room was hardly big enough for one, certainly not for two. As I sat on the foot of the bed, thinking and looking out the long window, I saw nothing but smoked-stained buildings heaving under the weight of time.

Less than twenty-four hours had passed since I left the familiar tin roofs of Glen Allan, the warm smoke curling from chimneys I had known all my life. There were no chinaberry trees, no pecan trees. The sound of Mama's and Ma Ponk's voices could not find their way through the maze of buildings that separated us. Never again would I pick dewberries or hear the familiar laughter from the field truck. This was my world now, this strange new family and their cramped quarters over the tiny corner grocery store they grandly called the "confectionery." I had grown up and gone north, all in one day.

As I unpacked the sparsely-packed suitcase and listened for sounds from downstairs, I kept telling myself that I would be all right, and I needed to say that. I didn't know where to hang my clothes; nothing had really been explained to me. I just kept taking things out of the suitcase and tossing them on the bed. As much as I might miss my family, I knew I could not go home. So many times I had said to myself that "Greenfield" was the end of my world and I needed more. Now I had more. St. Louis was more, it was beyond Greenfield and bigger than Greenville, the Queen City of the Delta. But St. Louis was a stranger just the same.

By the time I finished unpacking, I heard footsteps coming up the stairs. It was Aunt Clara. Aunt Clara had also come to St. Louis from Mississippi after learning that she had an older half sister here. She was very warm and, unlike Mama Beulah, went out of her way to make me feel at home. She had come upstairs to get the meal ready because today we would all eat together as my new life began. I laughed with Aunt Clara as she gestured about Mama Beulah's bossy attitude. She quickly put her finger to her mouth, pointed downstairs, and laughed softly as she walked out the door.

I knew then that I had made a friend. So I went about the task of acquainting myself by looking out of the much-needed windows.

I felt closed in by the bright floral printed wall paper that seemed anchored to the walls by the huge chest of drawers and the strange rubber plants growing out of milk cartons. I paced quietly and thoughtfully as I now tried to picture the little cousin whose bedroom I would share. Everyone else was downstairs in the store. I could hear customers coming and going and my new relations occasionally laughing as they went about their normal routine, interrupted by soft-spoken references to me, the new cousin upstairs. Upon thinking I heard my name mentioned I would strain to hear their conversation, but their muted voices were not able to ascend the steep winding stairs so I just kept looking at the lanky yellowish - green plants that seemed to be grasping for the sun. I knew that Mama Beulah would soon be returning, so I decided to sit down and wait. I was north now and grown; no familiar faces, no familiar space, just a room over a neighborhood store called a confectionery.

Recalling just a few days earlier back home in Glen Allan, I remembered being able to pace up and down Ma Ponk's hall when my mind was troubled and it seemed to help. Here, however, the little room was so crowded, I had no space to pace. At home I could look out the window across to Mr. Britton's field or out back where I could see as far as the colored cemetery, but now the old familiar acres and acres of fields were gone. Looking out the window of this small room, my mind was trapped by tall buildings that only reluctantly let the wind, rain and sun find space to blow the debris, and give life to the plants. I decided to rest on the bed, close my eyes and cherish the memories from home.

I paced and paced in my mind, talking to myself about this new life up north that was scaring me and requiring that I become an adult in about two hours' time. I recalled Ma Ponk's house back in Glen Allan, and my little cot that had the view from the two front room windows. The house and the room were small, but those two windows were my outlet to the world. I knew every inch of space in our old bedroom and even in the dark of night I could find anything I needed.

Nothing was ever moved and nothing ever changed. The iron bed in the middle of the room had the string from the light bulb tied to the head rail so that Ma Ponk could easily turn out the light after we were in bed. The chest of drawers that held her Sunday clothes and her good jewelry as well as the family pictures always served as a treasure trove for me. A little washstand that had belonged to her godfather stood near the foot of my bed, and oh how I loved the old wash stand. It was my place to keep all my collected trophies of youth. My rocks from the hills of Mississippi were there, as well as the old tintype photograph of an ancient relative, a few old Indian-head nickles, and my prized possessions, my bubblegum baseball cards. How I cherished those worn cards of Jackie Robinson, Willie Mays, and the men that comprised the Brooklyn Dodgers, the New York Giants, and the Cardinals.

My fond recollections of home were soon interrupted by the sound of footsteps coming up the creaky wooden stairs.

"I'm coming up. Hope you'se decent."

Mama Beulah, seeming somewhat tired from the trip upstairs, came into the small bedroom where I was sitting and waiting for my new set of instructions. She somehow seemed shorter now, not quite five feet as she stood in the arched doorway picking her gold teeth with the wooden toothpick which seemed to be her trademark. I watched as she opened the big trunk at the foot of her bed, humming all the time. She piled layers and layers of clothes on the bed until finally she found what she needed — a quilt. I watched as she gently and slowly pulled the brightly colored patched quilt from the bottom of the trunk. With her quilt in hand, she walked over to the center of the room and began to tell me about her older sister, Bessie, who still lived in the Mississippi Delta. As she talked about Bessie and the quilt, her face began to soften and her otherwise dark eyes began to light up.

"Bessie pieced this quilt for me. 'Course she'd send me one every year. But with my daughter and young nieces, I gave most of them away — except for this one, my favorite. It's the last one she made 'fore her eyes got bad. Look at the detail. I couldn't stitch like that if my life 'pended on it. 'Course she had time, down there in the South and all."

I would be given the chance to use this quilt until my folks sent me my own. It seemed as if the northern relatives looked to the receiving of those quilts as much as our southern relatives religiously pieced them year after year. Of course I was to use this quilt for top cover only, because as soon as I got my own, this treasure would be returned to the safety of the trunk.

As I held this piece of southern art in my hands I talked to Mama Beulah about closet space — of which there was little. It seemed as if all three of us would use the same built-in closet, making sure that we were careful not to wrinkle her good dresses — of which there were plenty.

As I continued to unpack my meager belongings, I tried to find comfort in the fact that I was North at last. But I had only been in St. Louis for a few hours, and had lived in Mississippi all my life. So all my memories centered around the home and the people that I had left behind. I was hungry, but still apprehensive about just barging into the strange kitchen. So after putting away the last of my belongings, I returned to the comfort of the small bed. It was hot in the city, so I wouldn't need the quilt for awhile, but as I held the intricately designed quilt, I felt for a moment that I was home. After all, the quilt was from the South.

Completely unpacked now and nowhere to go, I decided to go downstairs. While walking down the dark creaky stairs, I wondered, when would Ma Ponk piece me a quilt. She was getting old, but only last year, she had pieced two good quilts and one scrap quilt (no particular design). After all, I was up North now and I couldn't wait to get my very own quilt. As I slowly walked down the creaky and long stairs, it was beginning to dawn on me that I was truly up North. I was living in the city in a brick house with my bedroom upstairs. The stairs were dark but I could see the dim light from the store dancing on the bottom steps. As I stepped into the light and walked into the crowded confectionery I experienced a feeling of difference. Coming in and going out of the store were scores and scores of black people. They were ordering chickens, neck bones, liver, soap powder, and bunches of fresh greens. I stood there and watched as Aunt Clara checked out the customers, laughing and talking. They seemed to all know each other. With little space and no shopping carts their arms were filled. They didn't seem to care; they all talked to each other, gossiped and waited their turn.

Standing there in the dimly-lit store with packages and outdated goods hanging from the ceiling, watching Mr. Madison laughing and talking as he operated from behind the meat counter, I was reminded of Glen Allan and Hilton's Food Store where I had worked after school and during the summers. I laughed as I watched Mr. Madison trying to cut up a chicken and discuss politics at the same time. So without a second thought I walked over to the meat box and asked to cut the chicken. Still grinning, and talking politics, he wiped his hands on his apron and without breaking his train of thought, continued to talk politics while I became the butcher.

Having never met them, I would win their hearts with my southern work ethic. Mr. Madison, whom I later earned the right to call "Uncle Madison," became my ally as I soon learned to do every job in the small store from cutting meat to running the outdated cash register.

As the summer of 1963 passed I learned to be king of the confectionery and became the darling of all the little old ladies. Just like Uncle Madison and Aunt Clara, I would soon learn whom to let charge, whom to laugh with, and with whom to talk politics. I would meet Miss Missy, the seamstress, and Mr. Clyde, the numbers runner. I became part of the confectionery as more and more of their lives melded into mine.

I would learn to survive the small room and even get along with Michael — the new young cousin who was starved for a big brother. The boy never stopped talking and followed my every track. Clara and Sam would prove to be allies as we all worked together not to anger Mama Beulah. But it was

Sam's white Chevrolet that I loved, especially when it became my transportation for my first serious date. Mama Beulah was the boss, and fortunately I figured that out the first day. I paid homage to her as she delighted in her light skin and brown hair. Nearly seventy years of age, she was a liberated woman who smoked, played the numbers, and recalled with delight the loves of her youth.

But it was Uncle Madison and his style that really served as a model for the rewards of hard work and dedication even when an education was not part of the package. He had come north at a time when physical skills were in demand and he worked hard to make the most of it.

Yes, it was there in the company of Mama Beulah, the confectionery and the neighborhood people that I began the process of adjusting to the city. Even though it was small, I enjoyed working in a black-owned store that catered to the community. Because of my background at Hilton's Food Store in Glen Allan, I proved to be a valuable asset as I waited to get a "real" job.

Except for a few older white people entrenched in their homes, the neighborhood was all black. However, on those days when the Cardinals played at home, the streets were crowded with people of all races walking together and lining the small streets heading to Busch Stadium.

And as the summer heat took its toll we brought out all

the folding chairs and lined them up on the corner sidewalk. And we'd sit for hours watching the world go by. With time I would learn the people who had passed that corner for over thirty years; the old black men and women whose roots were deep in the South, but who had lived most of their lives in the city. I watched them as they hustled into the store or stood on the corner to catch the bus. Sometimes they would stop and talk to us, but most of the time they would just speak and keep moving.

It was a Saturday evening when I first encountered the numbers man in action. He was an old man, slightly gray, but he moved with the quickness of a trained leopard. At first, I didn't know what the whispers and strips of paper meant. I just knew that when Mr. Clyde came by, Mama Beulah would rub her hands together and her little beady eyes would get big as she shouted out, "I know I got the goods today." I'd watch as she moved from her seat out front where she held court, to right inside the door by the stairs. Mr. Clyde knew the exact next moves. Also watching his sides, he followed her into the little hallway and I overheard them talking and finally a laugh from Mama Beulah. I watched as Mr. Clyde quickly left and Mama Beulah came out grinning. She put her chair back out by the door and said, "The Lawd's been good to me." Later I would learn to laugh as Mama Beulah always looked to strike it big. She kept her supply of numbered strips—and if by chance a police car came by, she'd ball up the strips and give them to me to flush down the toilet. Late into the evening, enjoying the warmth and the brightness of the moon almost as if we were back home, the neighbors would sit out on their stoops, drinking beer, lying, and just having fun. The small store, somewhat reminiscent of Mrs. Florence's store back in Glen Allan, Mississippi, served as a rallying point for the people.

Twenty-six twenty-nine North Spring was not the North I had dreamed about as a child in Glen Allan, but it was my North, just the same. Aunt Dora, perhaps more than anyone, embodied the North of my dreams. Even though she had a very limited education, she had busied herself in being involved in church clubs and auxiliaries — and she didn't work. She was Mr. Madison's wife. She was as light as he was dark, and always the premier dresser. I had to prove myself to her, not one to open her heart to strangers at the first glance. But she would later learn to like me and of course credit that judgement to my good southern roots.

It was the last of August, 1963, and in less than three months, I had changed worlds. Settled into the confectionery, even using some of the skills learned while living in Glen Allan, I had now begun to call St. Louis home. But my days of adjusting would soon be over. I needed a real job and I wanted to go to college. I could see that life in the city would be different than anything I had dreamed, but I was ready.

CHAPTER FOUR

The Matriarch, the Church, and City Friends

C ity life was all around me, but I still felt like a country kid. That had to change. After all, I had come north and some form of transformation was absolutely necessary. I wasn't quite sure what would change first, whether it would involve clothes, hair style, or speech.

Somehow I had to acquire that style of city that we Southerners could always see, feel, and envy. But when and how would it happen? I could not go back to Glen Allan, Mississippi, until I felt I was a bona fide Northerner.

The first big change began for me the first Sunday in St. Louis, when I put on my best Sunday clothes and set out to find the Lively Stone Church of God. Despite my curiosity about my father's church, Hopewell Baptist, I had decided not to attend there. I had no desire to create friction for my father. Besides, the Lively Stone Church of God was famous; I'd heard about it even before I left Glen Allan. Sister Clay, one of my mother's friends who visited from St. Louis had told me, "If yore going to St. Louis, you gotta visit Lively Stone Church." Lively Stone had a Sunday night service which was broadcast live each week over KATZ radio. According to Sister Clay, that Lively Stone broadcast was the greatest thing about living in St. Louis.

All my life I'd gone to the little wood-frame, one-room church down the gravel road from Ma Ponk's house where a handful of colored folks sat on folding chairs and worshiped by the light of a single 60-watt light bulb hanging by a wire from the middle of the low ceiling. Lively Stone was a completely different experience. It was a cathedral, filled with hundreds of strangers who walked down carpeted aisles to sit on padded pews and worship by the light of gleaming chandeliers and stained glass windows.

When I arrived at Lively Stone that Sunday, dressed in

my Glen Allan Sunday best of a light blue wash-and-wear shirt, navy slacks, white socks and black shoes, my clothing couldn't have been more wrong for the setting.

My outfit and the bewildered look on my face must have made me stick out, because almost immediately a young man my age picked me out of the crowd, introduced himself, and set out to make me feel welcome. That young man, Mickey Piggs, gave life to the stained glass of Lively Stone, for he took me under his wing, introduced me to his family as well as his girl friend Ann Rowan and her family, and quickly became my best friend in St. Louis.

Mickey's parents had come from the Mississippi Delta. It never seemed to bother Mickey that I was from the country and had not yet mastered the social graces of the city. He just laughed and I said, "Don't worry about it; everything will work out fine."

And my friend Mickey became the man to emulate in my transformation to city ways. On Sundays, he was the epitome of the city man. Impeccably dressed with suit, hat, and Bible, he'd stop by the confectionery and wait for me to get ready for church.

"Mickey's here," Aunt Clara would call upstairs from the confectionery that never seemed to close, even on Sundays.

"Mickey, go on upstairs. You know the way," Aunt Clara would say to him.

My northern family quickly learned to trust Mickey who was always mannerly and respectful, qualities they liked and rewarded with their friendship. Receiving clearance to go upstairs, Mickey would virtually run through the confectionery's obstacle course, maneuvering around unpacked boxes, watermelons, and sacks of potatoes that Uncle Madison had unloaded.

"Hey! I'm coming up," Mickey would yell as he skipped steps and made his way up to the top of the stairs. Without fail, Mickey would be dressed in the latest suit and shoes. I'd come north without a suit. I would be hard pressed to match Mickey.

The first thing Mickey did was get me out of the white socks, into a pair of black ones that matched my shoes. But the real transformation would be much more difficult. By his well-dressed example, Mickey showed me that I was going to have to acquire a new suit. This seemed impossible, since I didn't yet have a job outside the part-time work I was doing in the confectionery.

At this point, another young man, a regular customer at the confectionery, let me in on a northern city secret. Realizing that I was suitless and virtually moneyless, this fellow pulled me aside and told me about a place operated by an old Jewish couple where they sold leftover sale suits, or suits with minor defects. Early one Saturday morning he gathered me into his car and away we went to a decaying section of St. Louis.

When we got to a rundown warehouse, we were met by an old, badly dressed man who recognized my friend and invited us in. Once inside, I saw an entire warehouse full of clothes — old clothes, new clothes, folded clothes, boxes of clothes — just laying on the floor or on tables in heaps and stacks. After talking with my friend, this rotund old man, with wild hair and glasses perched crookedly on his nose, came over to me and looked rather quizzically.

"Your size — what size suit do you wear? What color are you looking for?"

I had no answers. I didn't even know my size.

When I told him that, he just said, "Umph." I expected him to measure me. Instead, he picked up his half-empty Vess soda bottle and waved it nonchalantly towards the piles of clothing. "Go t'rough, find yourself somet'ing. I give you a good deal. I know your friend for years. He's a good customer."

It was the most unsightly mess I had ever seen, but somewhat exciting. For there in front of me were several small mountains of iridescent and sharkskin suits. I picked up a few coats and held them up to me. After about an hour of searching, I chose two suits that looked okay. Without question they were too big — but size was not a problem according to my friend. Miss Missy, who lived across from the confectionery in the only one-story bungalow on the street, was an excellent seamstress.

And that she turned out to be. It didn't seem to bother Miss Missy that the waistband was nearly twice as large as my waist and the coat hung on me like a drape with sleeves. A small plump lady with freckles and gray hair, she immediately had me try them on. And with her mouth filled with pins and measuring tape around her neck, she calmly, efficiently transformed me into a respectably-dressed Northerner. The suit, tailoring and all, cost me less than twenty-five dollars, and looked like it cost a hundred.

I remember the first Sunday morning I put my new suit on to go to church with Mickey. I had a big smile on my face as I walked out of the small bathroom. Mickey gave his nod of approval.

"How much that suit set you back?" he asked.

I walked over to the window and winked at Miss Missy's house. "Not much, Mickey, I got a deal," I replied as we both headed down the stairs.

With new pointed toe shoes, a new straw hat, black socks, and a suit remade by Miss Missy, I was now ready to go to church. It was beginning to happen — the style of the city was creeping into my life.

Aunt Clara went to her church, Hopewell, Uncle Madison stayed home to watch the store, and Mickey and I walked to Lively Stone. The streets were becoming familiar and I was feeling like I knew my way around — at least down St. Louis Avenue to where the church was located. As we got closer to Warner and St. Louis Avenue, I saw hundreds of well-dressed church people heading into the Lively Stone building which was reminiscent of a small Gothic cathedral.

On nearly every corner in the black neighborhoods, the large churches were the corporate example of northern success. While standing there with Mickey watching the people proudly file into Lively Stone, I recalled my first week in the city when cousins M.C. and Alberta took me out to show me the city.

Cousin Alberta was a Mississippian originally, but now a St. Louis resident for over three decades. As she and her husband drove me through St. Louis, they pointed out the black-owned funeral homes and successful churches, especially those pastored by former Southerners who also had come north.

Without question, I was impressed with what I saw. Alberta and M.C. would point out the site of an early storefront church. Then they showed me that same congregation's first brick building which became the foundation for their final move to the big-steepled church which was now their home. Upward mobility had happened and nowhere was it more evident than in the large black churches and the black-owned funeral homes.

My debut at Lively Stone as a well-dressed Northerner

that Sunday morning was filled with excitement. I was no longer intimidated by the size and opulence of the building, which was bigger, brighter, and prettier than any black church I had ever seen. All those hundreds of people had turned out to be friendly folks, many of them from the South. As Mickey introduced me to his friends, who later became my friends as well, I felt that these nicely dressed people were the Northerners that I would emulate.

True to the Lively Stone name, the church service was lively, and the preacher, District Elder P.L. Scott, soon became one of my favorites. I sat in his presence totally mesmerized by his oratory skills and ability to make the Bible come alive. Not unlike my preachers from home, he was athletic in his approach and did not hesitate to dramatize his sermons. Though much bigger and with a much broader vocabulary, he did remind me of Uncle Abe Brown, a preacher back home in Glen Allan. Uncle Abe had described life as a spider web with hell fire underneath. Our task was to walk the web as prescribed or suffer the consequences of the fury of hell fire. Elder Scott was not dramatic to that extent, but he stood over six feet tall, weighed well over 200 pounds, and dressed in black and crimson robes, so that his appearance and speech seemed equally as authoritative.

Lively Stone would become my church and many of these people would become the extension of the community

I had left behind. It was after those Sunday services that I would have the chance to visit the homes of many of the people who had come north during the twenties and thirties. They had come to St. Louis at a time when unskilled laborers were needed. Armed with their southern work ethic and eager to work and improve their lot, many of these men and women set out to defy the odds. Having left sharecropper homes and broken down shotgun houses, they seemed to have been committed to making the freedom of the North work for them.

The pride of their efforts was shown in their commitment to home ownership. Many of them had worked and saved to the point of having purchased "flats" that offered living accommodations for two to four families. Their income plus the income from their renters enabled them to purchase their part of the North. Proudly they would show me through their homes, through the separate eating areas and living rooms decorated with overstuffed furniture, as they recalled their own meager upbringing in the South. And no couple was more proud of their home than Uncle Madison and Aunt Dora. They lived on St. Louis Avenue. Aunt Dora, bursting with pride, showed me through each room, pointing out the nice pieces and attributing it all to hard work.

I had new clothes and new friends, but these were not all it took to make me a Northerner. Equally as important was finding a barbershop. One thing for sure, whenever I went south, it was important that my hair looked northern. Those of us growing up in Glen Allan could always tell a northern hair cut.

Back home, when I needed a haircut, I went to Mr. Will's. I recalled those reluctant visits to Mr. Will with maturing fondness, because a visit to the barber shop, a male environment, was like an informal rite of passage for a young man. There were two such establishments for colored people in Glen Allan, Mr. Will's makeshift home barbershop and Mr. Maxey's real shop. Both were places where black men and older boys talked religion, politics, and women. For me, Mr. Will's was the place to learn about life.

His barbershop was on his back porch during the summer and in his kitchen during the winter. Mr. Will and his wife Miss Henrietta (Ma Ponk's fishing buddy) were a team, she being very skinny and quick witted, and he overweight and balding with a laughter that made his round belly shake. He knew something about everything and so did his customers.

Coming through Miss Henrietta's front room which served as a living room and bedroom, and then through the kitchen, his customers would be welcomed by the smell of frying catfish, collard greens and sweet potatoes. It never seemed to bother his wife that we just came straight through and found ourselves a place to sit on the wooden benches that were crowded into the screened-in back porch.

You could hear their hearty laughter from the front door as the men talked about their week of work, their bosses and the prospects for the future. And all the woes of the white plantation owners would be discussed as well as the problems those owners were having with their children.

Too young to participate, I would just sit and listen as Mr. Will gave the final word on every subject. And when it was my time for a haircut, with no style book to guide him, he'd just set me in the chair, his conversation not interrupted. "I know your folk, they don't want much left on," he'd say as he went to the business of cutting my limited hair while his soft round belly served as a welcome cushion for my head.

I could tell when the conversation shifted from what I should hear to the Saturday night happenings. Mr. Will would say, "Hold that thought till this boy leave." Within a few minutes, my tight black curls would have joined piles of hair on the floor around the barber chair.

"O.K. boy," he'd say as I paid him my fifty cents.

He'd shake his towel and call for the next guy and I would again walk through his house headed home, only to hear them making guttural laughs as I closed the front screen door. One day, I thought to myself, I'll be able to laugh with the men.

Finding a barbershop in St. Louis was not a difficult task,

because there seemed to be one on every corner. But I wanted to find one with the warmth of Mr. Will's, but with definite northern skills. So I shopped around and finally settled on one about four blocks from where I lived. It was a real shop. The barber wore a white smock and the place had real barber chairs. Chairs for the men waiting to get haircuts were neatly placed around the walls. It was clean and white with cabinets filled with all kinds of tonics and hair cream. This was a *real* place, so unlike the ones back home. I was a bit intimidated at first, but my apprehension soon left as the regular customers began to file in. Before long, domino boards and checker boards were out, and the men began laughing, smoking, and lying. I relaxed. I had found a good spot.

The new barber was trim, not overweight like Mr. Will, but he had an opinion about everything, and when the conversation got around to women, no one said "Hold that thought."

With my hair neatly trimmed and lined, new friends, and new clothes, I was beginning to become one of them.

But I was still concerned about my speech. The ring in the voice, the placement of verbs, and the use of big northern words were very important to me. Down South we knew how to spot a real Northerner — by the sound of his voice. And I had spent many of my summer months as a child growing up being enthralled by the sounds from our visitors. We took our time talking down south, but a Southerner turned northern soon learned to speak faster. For some reason, they all seemed to have a vocabulary that outstripped ours. From "confectionery" to "tavern" to the pronunciation of "water," I just loved to hear them talk. I had thought that the change in speech must be part of the transformation that took place once the Mason-Dixon line was crossed.

And even though Mama Beulah, the undisputed matriarch of the Spring Street Confectionery, was directly from the South, she had perfected the art of becoming northern. With very limited education, she had managed to create an aura of style that defined the best of the North. It was on Sundays that Miss Beulah and her style would come alive. She dressed in a duster and slippers throughout the week, but Sundays brought out the corsets, the weaved hair, the fur stole, and the makeup. Once her dressing was completed, it seemed as if she immediately began to speak differently and with a "ring." Mama Beulah kept my hopes alive. For on those Sundays, she became like those I remembered coming home on the train, making their annual pilgrimages south.

Mama Beulah, Uncle Madison, and all the rest had made the transition. They had spent most of their adult lives in the city. They had their homes, and as it was among black folks in the South, the church provided them a welcome place for leadership. They were trustees, deacons, presidents of the Pastor's

Auxiliary and held scores of other offices that provided them a sense of upward mobility. And they all talked with a ring. Most of them had over thirty years of exposure to the North. How long would it take for me to talk like them?

For one thing, I had problems with the difference between lunch and dinner and the absence of supper. Everybody back home ate dinner around noon and supper in the evening, but not so in the city. No one talked about supper and as far as I was concerned they had misplaced dinner. After a period of time, I learned to adjust. And it was good that I did. One of my new friends from church, Oscar Guyton, Jr., invited me to his family's home for lunch — which I now knew to be dinner. Little did I know that this invitation would be the beginning of a lifelong family relationship.

Oscar Jr. was a first generation St. Louisian whose parents Oscar Sr. and Henrietta had come from the South. They too had left their homes in Mississippi, coming to St. Louis to build a better life for themselves. Even though they had left Mississippi, the best of the South they had retained. Their southern charm and sense of family were evident when Oscar and I walked to his parents' home on a street named Lincoln.

Lincoln wasn't very far from the church. I'll always remember walking to the front gate that led up to the small steps and porch that were part of the neat house with greenish

siding and a neatly trimmed yard. After a brief introduction,
I was shown the upstairs and the rest of the house. I was
overwhelmed by the Guyton family's friendliness as well as
with Oscar's room which he shared with his younger brother
Eddie.

Mrs. Guyton, whom I later earned the right to call Mom
Guyton, had prepared a simple family meal. Mr. Guyton also
welcomed me to their home and made me feel all right as a
Southerner. I watched as he "fathered" his family. His position
as provider, husband, and father was secure.

As we sat down to eat together in their small kitchen, I
felt the sense of family much like the days we sat on the screened
porch and ate with Poppa back home in Mississippi. Mr.
Guyton, his wife, his sons, his daughters, and their guest all
bowed heads as he blessed the food. Lima beans, fried chicken,
and macaroni never tasted better. They had welcomed me to
their table, a welcome that would eventually make me a part of
their life.

Oscar Guyton, Jr. became the close friend in whom I
confided my deepest feelings and fears. He and I would often
talk about my father and the fact that circumstances had not
allowed us to develop the relationship we both wanted. It was
Oscar who finally convinced me that I should at least visit my
father's church, Hopewell Baptist. I was afraid. I didn't want
to cause trouble for my father but I wanted desperately to hear

him preach. His reputation as an orator was nationally known, but I had never heard him.

I remember the Sunday evening that Oscar, much braver than I, decided to slip me into one of my father's services.

When we got to Wagoner Place, the church grounds were packed with cars, but we managed to find a safe place to park and quietly entered the church. So unlike the small churches back home, my father's church was rather large.. There were padded pews instead of folding chairs and the musicians were the best.

I sat there mesmerized as I listened to cousin Alberta sing solo. Alberta was one of the relatives my father had introduced to me. The gleaming chandeliers, the plush pews, the huge picture of my father at the front of the church, and the soulful sound of Cousin Alberta all melded together to give me a sense of pride. I watched the homage paid to the Mississippi orphan they all called "Pastor."

I wanted to be introduced, so I could say "This is my father," but I couldn't.

My father began to preach. He was better than any preacher I had heard before. He held the audience in the palm of his hand and gave them hope for a better life. As his sermon began to reach a crescendo, Oscar and I silently slipped out, never to return to Hopewell Baptist again.

My father was undoubtedly a star in St. Louis, but I had

to make my own way there. And it was beginning to happen as I learned the ways of the North: the walk, the talk, the dress, the hairstyle. There were services at Lively Stone, Sunday dinners, new friends, and even, perhaps, a change in my voice. St. Louis was home now, and I was beginning to fit in.

Vol. 86 No. 239   (86th Year)   © 1964, St. Louis Post-Dispatch   ST. LOUIS, SATURDAY, AUGUST 29, 1964—18 PAGES   PRICE 7c

AMAGE IS HEAVY
PHILADELPHIA
REET RIOTING;
ARE INJURED

ice Attacked—
res Arg Looted—
ruction Spreads
Large Area

CIVILIAN PREMIER
TO RULE SOUTH VIE
KHANH SAID TO BE

TURKEY AGREES
TO POSTPONE
ROTATION OF
CYPRUS TROOPS

Decision Made as
Situation
Headed for Shooting
Showdown

Scenes of Rioting in Philadelphia

This was the view this morning on Columbia avenue looking west from Fifteenth street after rioting last night and early today in the predominantly Negro area

of north Philadelphia. At left, firemen clear smouldering rubble from a store set afire by looters. The street is the area's main thoroughfare.

PRESIDENT MAPS

U.S. WILL ISSUE
FOUR CHRISTMAS
POSTAGE STAMPS

WASHINGTON, Aug. 28 (AP)
—Christmas mailers will have a
choice of four seasonal red-and-
green Scenl postage stamps this
year. The Post Office Department said it is the first time that
such a four-in-one issue had been
offered.

A buyer of a sheet of 100
Christmas stamps will get 25
stamps showing a sprig of holly,
the same number each of
mistletoe, pine cones and poin-
settia.

CHAPTER FIVE

Looking for a Real Job

I n the South we grew up knowing that we would work. Summers and weekends found me and most of my peers with virtually no vacation days, only work days. I never expected my life to be any different up North, and these expectations were very much to the liking of Uncle Madison and Aunt Dora. I made myself very busy in their small confectionery without them having to urge me. I once overheard Uncle Madison telling a customer that I was typical of boys

ST. LOUIS POST-

THURSDAY, JULY 11, 1961

NEGROES SHOUT JOB DEMANDS AT CITY HALL IN E. ST. LOUIS

200 Pickets Parade 20 Blocks, Then Hold Conference With the Mayor

About 200 hymn-singing Negroes paraded in front of the East St. Louis City Hall today to protest against the alleged failure of city officials to improve employment opportunities for Negroes.

The pickets, shouting "We want jobs now," gathered between 8 a.m. at Lincoln Park and paraded 20 blocks to the City Hall, at 607 Collinsville avenue, where Mayor Alvin G. Fields met with a committee of Negroes for about an hour. Fields agreed to meet them again at 10:30 a.m. Monday. Negro leaders said they would expect a progress report then, and that if it were not satisfactory they would ... and other demon...

Demonstration ... East St. Louis City Hall (J

coming up from the South, not afraid of work.

Even while busy doing all kinds of odd jobs at the confectionery, however, I knew that I must look for a real job. But St. Louis was so big. I had no car, the transit system was foreign, and the St. Louis expressways kept my heart in my mouth. Nevertheless, I knew that the time to look for a job had really arrived when I began to see seventy-year-old Mama Beulah reading the want ads. She was not very subtle in her hinting. She took to leaving that part of the newspaper conveniently in my path, and dutifully I also scoured the ads daily.

After looking them over, I busied myself again in the confectionery. I was intimidated by the sound of the jobs and their requirements. I had never prepared a resume, and I had very little office skill. I thought I had a lot to offer, but I wasn't sure if it was what the people advertising in the newspaper were looking for.

Still, I had a lot of hope. As the days drew into weeks, I began to feel the pressure of finding a real job. I was barely seventeen, yet to those in St. Louis, I was an adult. And with adulthood came financial responsibilities. The small income from my part-time help at the store was totally insufficient to meet my needs. And I had my dreams. I was determined to go to college.

Back home, you were born into field work without much

thought or action on your part. Mr. Walter's truck had always carried people to chop or pick cotton. No need to read the employment section of the Greenville Mississippi *Delta Democrat Times.* You knew your job, and so did everyone else. Even though there was a slight stratification of jobs, it was all manual labor. I had never before faced the fear of rejection that was crowding into my mind as a first-time Northerner. From picking cotton in Glen Allan, I moved up to oiling the wooden floors of the post office on my hands and knees. I'd gotten that job with Miss Johnson (the white postmistress) because my sister Claudette provided a family reference and my older female relatives had distinguished themselves as dependable housekeepers or maids. But my family tree mattered little to St. Louis employers.

Poppa wasn't there. Ma Ponk and the people of Glen Allan who had undergirded my life were hundreds of miles away in a world that I had chosen to leave. How I missed the assurance of their presence! In Glen Allan, I was somebody: Mary's son, Elder Young's great-grandson, and Miss Ponk's nephew. In St. Louis, I was just establishing a relationship with people who hardly knew me. Except for the smiles and greetings of the confectionery customers that I had gotten to know, the North was a city of strangers who acted and talked differently from this Southerner just up from the South.

Though I lived with good folks who had spent most of

their adult lives in the city, I knew that I was on my own. Rent would soon be due, and my commitment to send money back home was due as well. Without a doubt, I needed a real job that paid real money.

According to my new St. Louis acquaintances, McDonnell Douglas was the place to find a good-paying job. I knew McDonnell Douglas was a big place. It had been pointed out to me by my church friends as we drove around the city. It was big and scary and the expressway on-ramps and off-ramps you had to take to get there weren't very inviting. With most of my life spent on black tar and gravelled roads, I was not prepared for the rigors of city driving. I was scared to death of the St. Louis expressways. To some extent, I was glad that I didn't have a car, because without a car maybe they wouldn't expect me to fight the traffic to McDonnell Douglas.

According to the employment grapevine, there were jobs available in the paint shop that paid a good hourly wage. The wage was more than I had ever received. Everybody said I just had to go apply. I eventually gave in to their pressure. But I seemed to be getting farther and farther away from my own personal dreams. The fall would soon be here and the money for me to go to college was nowhere in sight.

I did not want a job as a painter. I had painted in Glen Allan. I recalled with cringing pain the week that seemed like a year when we had painted Mr. Carr's rent house in Glen

Allan. Mr. Carr was white, owned the grocery store, and lived in a new house on Lake Washington.

Located directly behind his well-manicured yard was a two room wooden house built from rough-hewn lumber, the type that drinks paint like water. My stepfather Moses had the habit of agreeing that "it ain't no problem," when anyone wanted a job done. Then, of course, I was drafted to be one of the problem solvers. There we were, father and son, standing on hand-made scaffolds turning this weather-worn shotgun house a bright green. I painted and painted and painted from early morning to late evening. Under my breath, making sure my father did not hear my thoughts, I swore that if I ever got off that scaffold, I'd never paint again.

Now here I was in my "promised land," being asked to paint for a living. It seemed as if my Tuesday morning appointment at McDonnell Douglas was a step backward, but I had no choice. I needed work, and "they" said that the money was good and the retirement benefits even better. Everyone in the little apartment over the confectionery was delighted with the idea of me being a painter at McDonnell Douglas. Mama Beulah fixed a big breakfast, complete with grits, eggs and bacon, and a large glass of orange juice. I was up, dressed, and ready hours in advance. Aunt Clara, who had gone downstairs to open up the store was equally ecstatic. Her live-in friend Sam stuck his head in the door to wish me good luck.

And I would need luck.

I wasn't sure what to expect and whether or not I could do the job. I was a scared seventeen-year-old Southerner trying hard to be a northern adult. By the time my cousin came by to pick me up, I had almost walked a hole in the pavement outside the store. We drove the expressways, fighting traffic all the way from the inner city out to the airport where McDonnell Douglas was located. As we drove I wondered if I'd ever be able to make this drive by myself. We got there on time in spite of the traffic.

I had never been in a personnel office before. Miss Johnson in Glen Allan hired me on the spot to clean the post office, and later Mr. Hilton had simply walked in the post office and told me, "I need help in my grocery store. You can start Saturday." No paperwork was involved. Even though I was now armed with a high school diploma and a valedictory sticker, I was still no match for the system of the city.

In the personnel office it turned out they wanted me to think "paint" forever. I talked to them about my dreams of going to college, but no one seemed to hear me. Or perhaps they did. For some reason, the personnel officer felt I was not the type of employee needed for that opening. Disappointed, we silently returned to 2629 North Spring Avenue to tell the sad news.

As we drew closer to Spring Avenue, I could feel my

mind searching for answers. What would I tell them? By now all the neighbors would know that I had gone out on this job interview.

As we pulled off the expressway onto the city streets, it seemed as if every building had grown taller and was now looking down at me, wanting to know the outcome. Even the little kids, who usually ran out into the streets totally mindless of people and cars, seemed now to be stopping and looking expectantly into the car. "It was only a painting job," I thought to myself.

As we silently drove back to 2629 North Spring I sat quietly, listening to radio station KATZ and recalling the weeks before I left home to go north when I had gone to see Poppa.

I really loved Poppa. All my Glen Allan relatives wanted me to be a teacher like my mother had been, and Poppa was no different.

As we sat on the garret, as he called the front porch, and ate caramel cake baked by his new wife, Miss Sissy, he talked to me about doing the right thing. Everybody said I'd do good up north cause I had "mother wit" and "book sense." Poppa told me I'd need them both up north. Of course I believed him. Poppa, Mama Pearl, and their daughter Rosie (my grandmother) had lived in Chicago for a brief period of time, but for some reason had returned south. Sitting there on the porch with Poppa I felt so secure.

Now, in St. Louis and out of a job, just remembering his words steadied my feelings. Yes, I knew I'd be all right up North, 'cause Poppa said so.

Everyone at the confectionery was disappointed that I had not been hired, but Mr. Madison said, "Oh the boy'll git a job. Just a matter o' time."

So, we survived the loss of the painting job. Mama Beulah, not one to let the trail get cold, immediately went back to discreetly placing want ads in places that would be obvious to my eyes. For my part, I always made it a point to have her see me with telephone and newspaper in hand at the same time.

I was now under a lot of pressure, and I felt I had no one to confide in. Certainly I didn't want the folks back in Glen Allan to know my situation. I finally told my new friend Mickey that I desperately needed a job.

I didn't know where Mickey worked, but I knew it was downtown and he seemed pleased with his job. One Sunday night after the church's broadcast, we discussed my job situation. It was that conversation that actually provided me my first St. Louis job as a dishwasher at Scruggs Vandervoots, a large downtown department store.

I never told my relatives down South the nature of my specific duty. I only said I was working downtown. Every day Mickey and I would dress in our suits and ties, and catch the bus to our job.

I was excited to get the job at Scruggs, not because I was washing dishes, but because Mickey and I could catch the bus together. Back home in Glen Allan, it had been easy to get to work. If it was too far to walk, one of the field trucks would pick you up. Here in the city, they talked transfers and shelters, all of which were foreign to me. My fears were easily handled by Mickey, for he had become a pro. Never one to be late for work, Mickey had me up bright and early. Both of us walked over to St. Louis Avenue and Grand to catch the bus.

I watched Mickey's every move from putting money into the slot to buying the transfers. I followed Mickey back to the middle of the bus which was filled with "colored" people. Here we got a seat, unfolded our copies of the *St. Louis Post-Dispatch*, and began to read. Sitting all around us were other workers all dressed neatly. Many were headed to semi-labor jobs, some of which they had held for decades. Getting off on Olive Street downtown, Mickey and I would quickly walk to Scruggs, where we would take the elevators downstairs to our lockers and change into our work uniforms. With our suits and ties secured in our lockers, we headed to our dishwashing jobs, dreaming of a day when we would not have to put our suits in our lockers.

While doing those pots and pans, I had plenty of time to think. Often I thought about Mr. Louis Fields who had encouraged me while I was growing up in Glen Allan. He had told me that I could be anybody I wanted — a doctor, a lawyer, or even an architect.

Now I saw my life being filled with grease and soap suds, and I knew that this was not Mr. Fields' dream. I washed those pots and pans with an intensity because I was washing my way out of that grease room. It would be months before I would leave the pots and pans, but I was determined. My family down South had dreamed of better things for me and I could not let them down. The stack of pots filled that washroom, but memories of southern voices crowded into that little room with us, and enabled me to look beyond.

Occasionally, I would get a break and I would peep out into the cafeteria and watch the throng of blacks and whites in line together. I would later learn that Scruggs lower cafeteria had not been too long integrated. Little did I know that, as I was watching the happy black Northerners slide their trays along with the whites, history was being made in front of my eyes.

But I will always remember the day the black opera singer Grace Bumby and her European husband and daughter came through the line. Time stopped. We all watched as this beautiful black lady and her integrated family filled their trays. As they were being served, I heard some of the white servers express their disapproval in her choice of a husband. Not me.

I had come north to see integration, and today I was seeing it at Scruggs.

As summer waned into autumn, Mickey and I would continue the ritual of dressing and bus riding and I would also keep visiting employment agencies, still keeping my fingers crossed for that "good job."

CHAPTER SIX

Quilts:
Kiver for
My Children

T
he winter of 1963 would not be unusually cold for those native to St. Louis, but it was to be my first "northern" winter, one of those winters that Ma Ponk and Ma Mae had often talked about. In order to get through that first winter, I would learn to dress warm with scarfs, ear muffs and lined gloves. And as the days got colder and the snow deeper, I would also learn to time the buses to the minute.

But more than anything, I would be saved from the cold weather by a box that arrived in mid-October from Glen Allan.

I had looked forward to getting a package from home since my arrival in St. Louis five months earlier. Every day I could not wait to get home from work to see if the mailman had brought me a package. And my waiting and hoping were not in vain.

I recall vividly the day I came home from work and Mama Beulah said, "Boy, you got a package upstairs from down south." Without stopping to do my normal chatting with the customers and the kin folk in the confectionery, I rushed immediately upstairs to my shared bedroom. There on the foot of the bed was a medium-sized box wrapped in brown paper and tied with white cord string. It was addressed to Mr. Clifton Taulbert and it was from Ma Ponk. As I untied the tightly-wrapped box with the brown paper glued to the sides, I laughed. I remembered Ma Ponk's insistence on wrapping her boxes tightly so that those nosey post office people up north would have no idea of the contents.

Excitement mounted as I untied the package and wondered if Ma Ponk had mailed the box herself or had gotten one of my sisters or my brother to walk uptown and mail it for her. I could hardly wait. I sure wanted some genuine southern pecans. Ma Ponk always included a four pound bag of big soft-shelled pecans when she sent her sons Melvin and Sidney their winter boxes. She had been sending winter boxes north for almost thirty years now. Quilts and pecans, and on those very rare occasions, a plain cake from her sister, Aunt Willie Mae, would be included. I had helped her fix and wrap and mail those packages every autumn. Now she included me in her list of those getting a package.

I sniffed as I hurriedly opened the box, but I couldn't smell a cake or hear a rattle. As always Ma Ponk had wrapped her packages well. She would save up piles and piles of *Sunday Delta Democrat Times* newspapers and stuff the boxes so tightly that only air would move. Nothing would rattle. At last I got the last knot untied, then I struggled to open the box which had been glued shut. Finally the flaps opened. I pulled out the piles of newspaper and reached into the box. Indeed there was a four pound sack of soft-shelled pecans, picked, I knew from experience, by Ma Ponk's own hands from the big tree in her back yard.

Then, as I pulled out the the sack of pecans, I felt the softness of material and I saw the start of a star, a brightly colored star. It was my quilt. Gently I pulled it from the box and laid it out across the bed. It was beautiful, Ma Ponk's version of the Star of David. The northern winters were said to be harsh, but now I would be prepared.

I hollered down the tall stairs, "Hey y'all, I just opened my box! You got to see my quilt."

As I inspected the quilt I thought to myself of the skilled labor which had gone into its making. It had no big squares, but lots of small pieces, neatly stitched together in the shape of stars.

The ladies of Glen Allan pieced quilts with a passion and my grandmothers and aunts were among the more passionate ones. I was Ma Ponk's collector of scrap materials that she gleaned from Mrs. Knight, the town seamstress, and from other members of the community.

A quilt from Glen Allan was truly from the community, for representative scraps of brightly colored cloth came from all over the little town. Dresses and pants no longer worn and Sunday shirts unable to be patched all became part of the scrap heap. Running through Glen Allan, I'd occasionally be stopped by Miss Sissy or Miss Stell who had saved bags of old clothes for the quilters. This collection of materials and scraps no longer needed would become the blocks and squares of flowers, birds, and patterned stars that would eventually be stitched together to form the top of the quilt.

As I sat holding my quilt from home, I recalled vividly the start of the quilting season. When the fall winds entered the Delta, the ladies' minds turned to quilting. It seemed as if those of Ma Ponk's household always started the rounds to gather scraps of cloth needed for quilting. Securely tucked away in the loft at Ma Ponk's were the quilting frames, wooden poles that had grown smooth from the scores of tired hands and the years of use. Always one to give me my orders, Ma Ponk would see that the frames were taken down and the hooks securely placed in the ceiling. She never trusted me to tie the poles, she always did that herself. Once the frames were set up there was hardly enough room to move around in the little parlor room, but soon the frames were covered with the start of the quilt, and encamped all around it would be older women who for years had followed this time-honored tradition. By the light from an exposed sixty-watt bulb and the flickering flames from the wood stove, I could see the ladies, bespeckled, tired, some of them dipping snuff. They had worked all week at other jobs, but they somehow found the creative energy needed to do the quilting. They hummed, gossiped, and talked to themselves as the patterns from their minds began to take shape. I was not allowed to sit in the room, but I would pass by the open door a thousand times, hearing the gossip not meant for my ears while seeing them working hard at a gift of love. And as the patterns grew and the gossip stopped, the quilts were pieced to the sounds of Dr. Watts' hymns, and the news from up north.

When fall ushered in the quilting season, the men of Glen Allan also had their traditions. Now facing a lull in the field work, they would go off with their #22 rifles to hunt rabbits, squirrels, and possums. They would leave early in the morning, heading for the woods, leaving the women to do the quilting.

Though hunting and quilting were both traditional autumn events, it was the quilting that carried the hearts of the people and the warmth of the South up north. According to those ladies of the South, our southern bones would never adjust to the cold of the North. Quilts were needed and nothing less would do. Prized possessions by both Southerners and Northerners, these designs from the heart and mind were always secured in trunks or large chests-of-drawers. Piles of handmade quilts were a status symbol, a show of industry, skill, and love.

Quilts were treasures to be envied and coveted. Even today, some thirty years later, I sometimes hear my mother and others discussing with dismay the disappearance of Mama Pearl's quilts soon after she died. Quilts were rarely ever sold, but always passed on from one generation to the next. Most often when the older black Southerners died, there was little or no money left. Much of the land had been lost, stolen, or sold. The greatest treasures they had to pass down to their children were the quilts. Soon after a funeral was over, friends and kinfolk of the deceased would gather for food and memories, and the traditional sharing of the quilts. Each quilt had its own particular story and the material used represented the times of that person's life, the joy and the sadness he or she experienced.

As a child in mid-Delta Mississippi I had been part of that time-honored tradition of quilting. Not only did I collect the scraps, but I helped to box and pack the quilts that would be sent north to our relatives. Without fail, quilts maintained the connecting link between the Southerners that went north and those that stayed behind. Now I had gone north and the connection was unbroken. Ma Ponk had sent me her heart and the warmth of my community. As memories flooded my mind I could hear the old people in Glen Allan saying, "Kiver up chile, it'll keep the chill out."

I remembered the old folks and clung to my quilt, until at last my new St. Louis family came upstairs from the confectionery to admire my aunt's handiwork, and perhaps silently compare the skills of their own southern relatives. And as they came up to see the quilt, we also shared some of my home grown papershell pecans. We cracked the pecans with our teeth, savored their meats, and admired the beauty of the quilt. For those few moments, we were all back home.

Left alone again, I looked out the window, across Spring Street at Miss Missy's house. I knew that snow would soon cover all the debris of the summer. I held my "kiver" close to me and I smiled inside. At last, I had my quilt, and I could give Mama Beulah's back for storage in her trunk. "I'll use it tonight," I said as I folded it again and laid it across the foot of the bed.

My first winter turned out to be all that Ma Ponk and Ma Mae had told me. It seemed as if all the snow of my life had come down to greet me. There were drifts of snow higher than cars, blown up by a chill wind that cut straight through to your bones.

The winters of the South had seemed like a gentle intrusion into an otherwise intensive labor environment. Here in the North, however, the winters were brutal. Ma Ponk had warned me that the people up north did not keep their houses warm. Instead, they dressed heavily throughout the winter. The control of the thermostat in the living quarters above the confectionery showed the truth of Ma Ponk's fears. At night the heat all but disappeared. There were no green logs to throw into iron heaters and no buckets of coal to keep the fires going all night.

I was prepared to face those northern nights warmly covered with the stars of David pieced together by loving hands and made soft with matted cotton from the scraps left over by the field hands. This would be one of two that I would receive from down south, where quilts were the kiver that kept us warm.

CHAPTER SEVEN

Driving Mr. Ross

E ven though I had only been in St. Louis for a few months, it had seemed like years. So much seemed to be changing so fast, both in my personal life and in the world around me. The war in Vietnam and racial unrest in the cities were dominating the news. Even though the winter months had brought a facade of quiet to St. Louis, my first Christmas in the city found us all still reeling from the death of President Kennedy.

Most blacks had felt Kennedy was their president, and for us, many hopes died the November day in 1963 when the president was assassinated. I remember that awful moment when Aunt Clara screamed out, "Oh, Lawd, they done shot President Kennedy." Everybody in the Spring Street neighborhood cried as we all kept vigil together. For those hours that lasted a lifetime, we all prayed for a miracle . . . a miracle that didn't happen.

Through the autumn and winter, Mickey and I continued to ride the bus each work day. Meanwhile, I diligently poured over the want ads in the evenings. I was determined to find a job that afforded me an educational opportunity.

While back home in Glen Allan, I had observed the social changes that were taking place. Vibrant, brave, and passionate voices were rising up and challenging the 'ole south' with its societal practices that had for years kept the races divided and economic progress for blacks at a snail's place. But it was here in St. Louis, where I had dreamed there existed an integrated life full of opportunity, that I saw the results of years of benign neglect clashing with the unfulfilled dreams of third and fourth generation urban blacks. Feeling their political muscles, while being taught a new concept, "Black and Proud," St. Louis blacks were beginning to bring their feelings to the streets.

I had come north looking for a better life. What I found was the Civil Rights Movement of the 60's in full swing. While in Glen Allan, my small agrarian community, I was isolated for the most part from the Civil Rights Movement that had begun to happen in the larger southern cities. I had heard about the demonstrations, the sit-ins and even the marches for voting equality, but I had not personally experienced anything of the movement and I hardly expected to find it in the North. St. Louis and the evening news brought me face to face with reality. Night after night we sat glued to the television sets watching as young men and women were beaten and jailed. The streets of St. Louis had become a showcase of their frustrations over the unfulfilled promise of integration.

Older black St. Louisians questioned the boldness and daring of their children who were challenging the establishment at every turn. But the young people were turning the tide of history, as they rallied around such rising black leaders as William Clay.

Of all the demonstrations, I'll always remember best those held in protest of Jefferson Bank and Trust hiring practices. For days young people laid in the streets in front of the bank, stopping traffic and requiring the assistance of the law enforcement officers. Even though I understood the thrust of their struggle, I was puzzled that blacks in St. Louis and my native Mississippi were both demonstrating for the same things. Mickey, my family, and most of our friends spent our days and evenings listening to the news, discussing the war, the riots, and the demonstrations that were taking place in the city.

Meanwhile, I had won the admiration of my employers at Scruggs. Even so, I was determined to find the 'northern' job I dreamed of. Responding to ads when I could had proved fruitless. Finally, in desperation, I found an employment agency that took me on as a challenge. Careful not to interfere with my dish washing job, they began to get me interviews. I was afraid, but I accepted the challenge.

And as I went from job interview to job interview, I began to understand the St. Louis protest movement. Much of commercial St. Louis had left black St. Louis behind. Nevertheless, I found a friend in one of the white counsellors at the agency and together we determined to plot a course that would change my future. Little did I know that he would send me to interview at Jefferson Bank and Trust, the object of massive demonstrations. For weeks and months, I had watched as the black youth of St. Louis called to task the management of this bank. Certainly I had never pictured myself applying for work there. But my counsellor had other ideas, and he scheduled the interview. While I passionately washed pots and pans at Scruggs, I thought about my upcoming date with the vice president in charge of personnel at Jefferson Bank. In my mind, I was ready for a real 'northern' job, and to me, nothing could be more northern than banking. The more I thought about it, the more Jefferson Bank and Trust became my goal. Even though the bank was in the news nightly for its reported refusal to give equal opportunity to blacks, my employment counsellor and I somehow felt that I could get hired. I remembered my first real job in Glen Allan at the Hilton Food Store, how I had won that job and kept it based on my ability, when my color might have disqualified me. The Hilton experience gave me courage to work with the agency and apply at Jefferson Bank at a time when getting hired seemed almost an impossibility.

I was not applying for a major position at the bank, but I recall that I was put through a battery of tests and interviews. Perhaps the bank always did this, or perhaps it was done in my case as a way to appease the employment agency and still disqualify me for the job. To everybody's surprise, however, I passed all tests. At the end of the long process, I was hired.

I was placed in the position of a bank messenger. This was an entry-level job. The first day at Jefferson Bank and Trust set the tone for my feelings throughout my short career. For the most part, the people were nice, but I recall with great clarity the day I was introduced to my supervisor, a retiring guard. He was a fixture at the bank — old, white, and perceiving himself to be part of the structure. He welcomed me, but made sure I understood my place. The job required that I wear a navy blue messenger uniform and adopt the servile attitude that he suggested be displayed for the customers.

The messenger cap, the pants with the satin stripe, the heavy buttoned coat with epaulets, all reminded me of the South and the work environment I thought I had left behind. Perhaps if training for future promotion had been part of the package, I would have enjoyed it. But I was simply a messenger and nothing more. I wanted badly to work inside the bank, but for the time, I stood at the door, opening and closing it for customers. Outwardly I smiled, but I was determined that I would never, ever let the uniform get inside of me. From my vantage point, as I opened and closed the heavy glass doors, I could see the vice president of personnel at his desk and the other vice presidents. Many were close to my age. I wondered if they had graduated high school at the head of the class, and if they had been given the opportunity to go to college. It wasn't so much that I envied them. I just always pictured myself inside at one of those desks instead of outside, holding the door and picking up trash. I had been glad to rake leaves in Glen Allan, but then even my white employer had dreamed of better for me.

I did not want to be them, but I knew that an inside desk was mine, and I was determined to do more than transport the money (checks) from the bank to the Federal Reserve. One day I saw a notice on the bulletin board that classes were being offered by the American Institute of Banking and all employees were invited to attend. Immediately I accepted the challenge. I fought the system the best I knew how by enrolling in school and doing exceptionally well.

Meanwhile, the family at the confectionery was very excited. To them, I was a banker. Uncle Madison was especially proud of my new job. I would watch with pride as this big black man, mostly bald, with a gold tooth and a boxer's build, would stick his hands in his pockets and repeat the story to anyone who would listen:

"Yes sir, Cliff 'straight from the South, and he gets a job at the bank. A Mississippian has something in them—there's people here been trying to get on for years, but our Cliff gets the job. 'Course I knew it all the time. That boy got something in his head plus mother wit."

The story grew by the hour as Uncle Madison told it, and everyone from Miss Missy the seamstress to the numbers runner was soon congratulating me on my new position. They had seen me come from having nothing to having a job that would be secure for the rest of my life until my retirement. Pleased though they were, I was not interested in retirement. I was still determined to see all my dreams come true.

Recalling the night of my high school graduation, I knew that my life had just begun. My teachers and family in Glen Allan had high expectations for me, and so did I. On that warm night in May 1963, as I stepped onto the stage to give my Valedictory address, I had told my classmates, "Our future is before us." I knew that my life and dreams were intricately tied to my community of Glen Allan, where the older people had invested their dreams in my generation. Those remembered voices from Glen Allan continued to encourage me to look beyond the messenger job, the uniform, and the potential pension, and to hold onto my dreams.

I started taking night classes at the St. Louis chapter of the American Institute of Banking, and it was here that I had my first integrated educational experience. White schools and white students were something of a mystery to the African-American children of Mississippi. Except for notes and jokes that we read in the used textbooks they passed on to us, we had little knowledge of their school behavior. But their writing and the scribbling in their books had sounded a lot like us. Now I'd be right there with them in class, answering the same questions and being given the same tests. Could I meet the challenge?

On those school evenings after work at the bank, I joined the "suits" who were trying to move further up the ladder. I wasn't on the ladder, so I had to really jump high just to reach for the bottom rung. As I held my "Principles of Banking" textbook, I felt as if I were really making that jump. Perhaps there was a world of difference between the "suits" who worked inside and the "uniforms" who worked outside, but the instructor, an inside banker, never asked questions about my specific job. Had he asked, I might have admitted that even in the life of a bank messenger, there were a few exciting moments.

Part of being a messenger required that I drive the president of the Jefferson Bank to appointments and to lunch. I still marvel that Mr. Dillon Ross, the president, would place his life in my hands in St. Louis traffic, when he wouldn't trust me with a calculator. Little did he know I had learned to drive on Mississippi turn-roads and knew nothing about cars. Traffic jams scared me. But every day without fail, I'd climb behind the wheel of the bank's company automobile to run interference through the downtown streets of St. Louis. There I'd be in my trusty blue uniform sweating for life while Mr. Ross sat confidently in the back seat reading the *St. Louis Post Dispatch* or the *Wall Street Journal*. He never once questioned my skills. Occasionally I'd put on the brakes too hard and he'd lean forward. Then we would both blame the other driver.

For almost one year I worked at the bank, attended school, and drove Mr. Ross to the St. Louis Playboy Club for lunch. I made straight A's and spent my time making a few friends within the bank. Even though race relations were a bit strained, some of the whites sided with my dreams and supported my efforts to get into the operational side of the bank. However, it appeared to me that the management of the Jefferson Bank seemed bent on not bringing black Americans into their front offices. There was one exception, Ernie, the messenger before me. As a result of the protests, he was moved inside. Many times at lunch Ernie and I would sit and talk and discuss the rationale of the bank's position.

Somewhat perplexed and confused, I found myself in a changing city. The youth of St. Louis were challenging their parents' way of life. Even haircuts, once conservative and clean-cut, were now a matter of controversy.

Guided by the conservative order of the fundamentalist church I attended, I did not consider myself personally involved in the struggle. Those of us who were part of the fundamentalist church continued our lives of church attendance and clean fun, careful not to agitate the church hierarchy by becoming involved in the demonstrations.

But I wondered, where was the North I had heard about while growing up in Glen Allan? Those summer visits from our northern relatives seemed now to have been carefully orchestrated theatricals in which the players spoke, dressed, and behaved as I wanted. Ma Ponk, Ma Mae, and the other seasoned travellers had further fueled my imagination by verifying for me that they, too, had seen that dream world and it was wonderful. Yet, apart from the magical ride on the train and the ornate vastness of the St. Louis train station, most of what I had encountered was markedly different from what I had been promised.

The winds of war, college unrest, the assassination of a president, and the demonstrations for equal opportunity framed the real world that had now become my home. I spent my days working at the bank and helped out in the confectionery on the weekends. What little spare time I had was spent listening and watching as many of the northern youths were hauled off to jail during protests. Violently and peacefully they had told us that all was not well in the North, and I knew they were right. I had not seen the black and white kids playing idyllically together as I had been promised. Except for a few whites, too old to move and perhaps having nowhere to go, my street was completely black. The city had moved away slowly to the suburbs, and those who remained behind were older and less affluent and, perhaps, had no desire to leave their beloved city streets.

The black folks who lived in the city seemed to enjoy the fumes and the busy street corners where they met, talked, and made city life happen. This was something akin to the closeness of their southern roots. The numbers man had become their friend and their passion for commerce had been visibly displayed on nearly every corner in the churches they had built. The bus routes were not difficult and the family shops and funeral parlors were visible signs of the success of the older generation.

At the confectionery, as small and inefficient as it was, there existed a sense of pride, of achievement. However, it was there on occasion that I would hear them say, "Yeah, guess who move to Florissant," or "They' movin' out to St. Ann's." Even though these people were 'north' to me, many of them were still moving in search of their dreams, north of a new Mason-Dixon line. I had taken the train north to a region in transition and no one had bothered to tell me.

I learned to play the game. My own letters south were not

much different than the scores of letters that Ma Ponk had received from family and friends over the years. I, too, painted a grand picture of differences. They never knew the size of Uncle Madison's store, nor did I bother to tell them about the projects, where the quality of living, though framed in bricks and glass, was really no better than in the southern shacks we had left behind.

The evening news and the *St. Louis Post Dispatch* both served to remind me that 'change' was inevitable and my life would not be as predictable as those generations who had come north before me. The Vietnam War had begun to escalate and the black communities were emotionally and physically involved. As more and more deaths took place, riots escalated. Black youths would never again be content with the mere illusion of equality.

At the confectionery where the old timers met, they all had an answer. They blamed the troubles on the assassination of President Kennedy. According to them, had Kennedy lived, the war would have been over, students would be studying, and businesses would be hiring fairly. If only they hadn't shot Mr. Kennedy.

Even though I had not given it much thought, the war and the student unrest had begun to trouble me. Young men from our circle of friends were being drafted daily. The war was for real and we were watching it from the comfort of our living rooms. While the young men of the city questioned the war's legality, the "old" men of the confectionery were speaking their minds as well. Some of these men had served in World War II and the Korean Conflict and were proud of their involvement. Now they too watched from the sidelines as the young men ushered in a new era of debate.

While the unrest in the cities and the war loomed heavily over us, my young friends from Lively Stone Church and I spent our Sundays at Lambert Field, the St. Louis Airport, enjoying simple pleasures like watching planes take off and land. Elder Scott, our Pastor, (a Mississippian himself) had managed to convince us that the church was all we needed and that the "world" would rob from us our commitment to the Lord.

With Elder Scott's admonitions ringing in our ears, we glanced nervously at the rousing St. Louis night life, but retreated to our world when faced with the decision.

My friends Oscar Jr., James, the Ramsey girls, Betty Battle and I would all pile into cars after church and head out to eat, expecting to have fun, but careful not to enjoy the frivolous things of the world that our church had warned against. Though limited activity was available, we compensated by becoming the best of friends. We thoroughly enjoyed the music of the church, while secretly becoming attached to the rising sounds of Motown.

Now, having friends my own age, I began to turn my attention to the prospect of serious dating. I didn't have much going for me, since I didn't own a car, had little knowledge of the city, and wore homemade suits. Still, I began to listen to my friends regarding the available female prospects. There were a couple of girls — or rather city women — who lived in my neighborhood. We had talked a time or two, and I had even been invited up to one of the girl's homes to listen to records. This was a definite "no no" for a member of one of St. Louis' premier fundamentalist churches.

To be safe, I felt I had to date a girl from church. There were fairly good prospects at Lively Stone Church, but I used most of my limited skills to pursue Betty, who was clearly out of my league. Then, one Sunday, a new girl showed up at church. Oscar, James, and I agreed that I would ask the new girl out. I was petrified. This lady was major league. Each time I thought of asking, I could hear my Mississippi cousin Bobby Fulton taunting me.

During my senior year at O'Bannon High School, the high school for country "coloreds," I had met a classy girl, Delores, at church. Delores went to Coleman High, the school for the city coloreds. Not only was she pretty, but she was a real city girl. I was not in her class socially, but her mother liked me and she finally consented to let me take her to a Coleman High basketball game. While we were enjoying the game, my cousin

Bobby Fulton showed up. Bobby was a city boy. When he saw me with Delores, he pulled me aside. "Cliff, you' way outta your league. This Delores chick is prime. How did you meet her?"

I had been intimidated by Bobby, and never told him I'd met Delores at church. Now, as I prepared to date this new "church" girl, Janice, I once again felt the disapproving presence of Bobby hanging over my shoulder, telling me that I was "outta my league."

But the memory of Bobby lost out. Janice and I did agree to a date, my first actual date in St. Louis. Sam from the confectionery loaned me his car, a 1964 Chevrolet, which was usually filthy but reliable. I set about cleaning out the car, getting out of it — and off of it — several layers of dirt. It was a long and difficult process, but by the time the evening for my date finally came, Sam's vehicle had a totally new look. For one thing, it was white. You would never have guessed.

Sam had given me so many instructions about the car that I was determined to start this date at one of St. Louis' drive-in eating places, and then to try and work my way to the park. Going on a date back home had been easy. Except for major school events, all the nice places were closed to "coloreds," so there was never anywhere to go. I was virtually unfamiliar with driving a car on a date.

But I ventured forth with all the daring I could muster.

I knew I was indeed out of my league, but that was the way I liked it. Since the voice of Bobby Fulton had followed me to St. Louis, I was determined to prove I could manage to stay out of my league, even here.

I took my date for hamburgers at White Castle, then we went driving through the park near the Natural Bridge. Both of us were chaperoned by the stringent rules of our church, but I was also chaperoned by the many admonitions I'd gotten from Sam. I made it a point to stay as close to him as possible with his car. As we enjoyed the coolness of a St. Louis night, the latest Motown sounds poured from the car radio, which Sam kept tuned to station KATZ. I figured Elder Scott could never fault me if Sam's radio happened to be on and playing Marvin Gaye while we were riding in his "unsaved" car.

We had a great time on that date. Still, I knew that Bobby Fulton was right. I was out of my league. My time in St. Louis would find me continuing this pattern. In fact, my attraction to the classiest women would continue through the rest of my life, becoming ever more evident, and culminating in my marriage to Barbara, who was, and still is, out of my league.

Those dates and Sunday outings with church friends to eat and watch planes land and take off would later become memories of great significance. I would look back and recall with great detail the amount of money we gave White Castle, my first real date in Sammy's 1964 White Chevrolet and the many Sunday afternoons when our choir was a guest at another church. Still, the church could not escape the change the sixties brought about. Lively Stone Church, fundamental and conservative, would see its posture changed as the term eventually moved from "colored saints" to "blacks" and as the hairstyle of the men and women brazenly became full and Afro-centric. A few would leave the church, moved by the social revolution to become part of the demonstrations and social change. I had come north at a time of dramatic change, and neither the North nor I would ever be the same.

So much had happened within a short period of time. I had washed dishes for a living. I had made the best of friends. I had watched the Guyton family as they made me feel at home. I had made Uncle Madison proud when I got my job at the bank. Miss Missy had made me new suits from old and I was attending the St. Louis chapter of the American Institute of Banking.

My grades were good, but my frustration with the bank grew by the day. I wanted a desk job. As I continued in school and applied for positions that never came my way, my friends encouraged me to hang in there. They felt sure that within a short period of time, I'd be brought inside. However, we will never know if management at the Jefferson Bank would have recognized my skills, because the war in Vietnam escalated and I would eventually change uniforms.

WANTING IN—Would-be voters lined up outside Circuit Clerk's office at Greenville yesterday—as elsewhere in Mississippi—waiting to register in the wake of enactment of a Federal voting rights law relaxing voter registration requirements.

CHAPTER EIGHT

"The North 'Grees Wid You"

August 20, 1963

Dear Cliff,

How are you. We are all fine. It is real hot down here. Your momma and the children are good. Take care of yourself. Be good. Try to find Lucille. Tell her to write me.

Your Auntie
Elna Peters Boose

For months the letters came from Ma Ponk, my mother, and occasionally from my sisters and brother. And with each letter, I wanted more than ever to go home. Part of the attraction of being north was being able to return south on the Illinois Central. This had been my dream as long as I could distinguish between north and south. I wanted to go north and return home. As a kid, I loved going with Poppa or Ma Ponk to the train station in Greenville. It didn't matter to me that it was segregated and we were kept to one side of the depot. I just revelled in the excitement and grandeur of the surroundings. We would clean out the car, dress our best, and drive to the station in Greenville. Then, we'd sit, stand, and stand some more until we heard the whistle and sound of the engine coming through Metcalfe. And we knew behind those small train windows were our people, all dressed up, coming from up north. The excitement would mount as the train stopped and the porters got off and stood by the doors. Then the passengers unloaded, and suddenly we'd catch sight of one of our relatives, who would begin to wave and cry. No matter how anxious they'd been to leave the South, when they returned home, they always cried at the train station.

The returning relative would be inspected from top to bottom.

"Where's your weight?" Ma Ponk would first ask. "Ya'll just don't take care 'o yourself up north. You eat all that funny food. But don't worry," she continued, "we take care 'o that. We got plenty good food. Greens, fresh pork, and Willie Mae, lawd, has cooked more sweets than ever. So good to have you home!"

The relatives would rub my head and say, "Little Cliff, I can't believe you are Mary Esther's little boy." I never answered, I was being talked about, not talked to. Nevertheless, I enjoyed the excitement.

And this was the scene I wanted to repeat. I wanted to be well dressed, with the right sound in my voice. I wanted to have them at the station waiting for me.

I wanted to cry. I had been saving those returning- home tears all my life. I wanted them to make a fuss over me. I wanted to hug and kiss them. I wanted to get my face lost in the smoke from the train. I, too, wanted to have money so that I could give some to a little cousin to polish my shoes. I had wanted to go north so badly, but I wanted to return home for the first time even worse.

But I could never repeat the scenes I had dreamed. The Illinois Central had stopped serving Greenville. I was shattered when I heard the news. I could never make this portion of my childhood dreams come true. I would never have the joy of confidently walking down the aisle to take my seat by the window and watch my hometown slowly come back into my life.

I couldn't afford to fly and I had no car, so my only other source of transportation was the Greyhound bus. I knew the bus would get me home, but never in the style provided by the train.

Still, I couldn't wait to go home. A lot of preparation had to take place. Presents had to be purchased. Letters had to be written. My vacation schedule had to be cleared with my supervisors at Jefferson Bank. With anticipation and guarded fear, I prepared for my first trip back to life behind the Mason-Dixon line.

We all knew that the South was changing. The Civil Rights Movement and Dr. Martin Luther King had begun to pull the people together as they prepared for a new day.

Glen Allan and one of her favorite sons, Mr. Jake Ayers, would become part of the movement that would forever change the face of my south. Historical mountains were being challenged, and leaders were rising up from the people. As I watched St. Louis wrestle daily with the questions of rights and equality being posed by her black citizens, the way of life I knew as a Mississippi colored child had also begun to crumble.

Regardless of the uncertainty I would face, I still had to go home. The anticipated joy of seeing family and friends outweighed any apprehensions I may have had.

The day finally came for my bus trip home. Loaded down with presents I couldn't afford and overdressed for a bus ride, I was more than ready to head south. I could hardly wait to see Ma Ponk and my mother, and to visit Poppa. I looked forward to a visitor's dinner at Ma Mae's house.

Though the bus ride was uncomfortable and crowded

and stops were made at nearly every small town, we finally arrived in Greenville. Looking out the bus window, I saw family — my oldest sister Claudette, Ma Ponk, and my mother. They were all smiles and I couldn't wait to feel their arms around my neck. Claudette was never one for much talking, but I think she was glad to see me. My mother and Ma Ponk were happy to the point of tears. We got my luggage, loaded it into the trunk of the car, and headed south down Number One Highway to Glen Allan.

As we passed the old Greenville train depot, I looked with silent nostalgia at the lovely building that had once been the hub of activity. Today, the wood-framed building looked dreary, weighted down with memories from another era. There were no trees. Debris had found a home where well-dressed people once stood. I glanced at the railroad tracks as we passed by. They too had begun to rust; their long rails which had once been covered with grease were now dull. Johnson grass grew nervously wherever it could between and around the unused rails. The platform where once the conductors and porters held court now served as a meeting place for the pigeons who had come to call the old station home.

Except for the demise of train travel, nothing much seemed to have changed in Greenville. Yet everything felt strange. Perhaps it was just that I had changed. I figured I would know better when I got home to Glen Allan.

We proceeded down Number One Highway. Claudette was driving, and she got plenty of back-seat assistance from Ma Ponk. I was sitting up front watching everything we passed.

As we went by Reed Road, I recalled those many days when our school bus had made that right-hand turn taking us to my high school, O'Bannon High. Even though we passed two white high schools on the way, we had to go to the western line district that had the designated high school for the "coloreds." Every school day for four years we would make the hundred-mile-round-trip to and from school, stopping in Glen Allan and at all the little plantations in between. Reed Road had not changed and I doubted that O'Bannon had changed. Mr. A.T. Williams was still principal, and my favorite teacher, Millicent Jackson, was probably still teaching biology and encouraging her students to dig deep and bring out their best.

In between spells of back-seat driving, Ma Ponk asked me questions. "Did you find Lucille? I know she's there. 'Course the last time I talked with Callie, Percy had said Lucille was doing quite nicely. But that gal, good as she is, left home and ain't been back. That just ain't right. No sir. No matter where you go, don't ever lose touch with home."

I had indeed located our lost cousin Lucille in St. Louis. She and her husband lived on Penrose. After tracking her down through an outdated phone number and address, I called her and made her remember my mother Mary Esther who was her good friend. She remembered right off and invited me over to her home. Like so many of our relatives and friends, Lucille was among those who left the South in the late thirties and never returned home, not even for funerals. They had purchased one-way tickets north and for many of them "home" would be a place they remembered in their minds, but never visited.

They were not forgotten in the South. Their names, the names of their families, and little bits of their lives were always mentioned. They may have gone north via the Illinois Central, but the family in the South kept them in their hearts.

"Ma Ponk," I answered, "I found Lucille and she was real nice to me. She made me a big dinner and told me to come over anytime. We even went together to church a few times. I asked if she were ever gonna come back home, and she just said 'No'."

Ma Ponk smiled and nodded. "I know'd if you found her she'd treat you good. Lucille's Mama raised her like that. Jest 'cause she's gone north, ain't meaning she forgot her training. Bet she fixed you mo' than salad. I know you had a good meal there. But lawd, I'd sho' like to lay my eyes on that gal. You know her daddy was Mama Pearl's younger brother. Good blood."

We talked on about Lucille, Alberta and M.C., and some of the others who were now Northerners, and Ma Ponk seemed pleased to hear about the family. But she was like that. She kept up with the family, no matter where they had moved and how questionable the relationship. According to Ma Ponk, "Blood is blood."

All the little plantations between Greenville and Glen Allan were still there. We passed Foote, Marathon, and Wildwood. When we got to Wildwood, I asked about Willie Reed. Willie was tall, black, and always keeping us in laughing stitches. Ma Ponk knew his grandmother, Miss Matilda. No one knew for sure where he was now, but Ma Ponk had heard Willie joined the Army. It was hard to picture Willie Reed in the military. I remembered him most for the night we all performed in a talent show at the Moore's Elementary school, formerly Glen Allan Colored School. As lanky as he was, Willie had insisted on being Elvis Presley. With an electric guitar and a black wig that dripped with perspiration and grease, Willie shook us all to the then-popular tune of "Jail House Rock."

With Wildwood behind us, we were just minutes from Glen Allan. Driving through Glen Allan's one main street brought back floods of memories. Mrs. Knight was still the town seamstress. I wondered who was raking and bagging her fig leaves. I had spent many Saturday mornings raking her yard and sharing a noon meal at her table in spite of the social restrictions of the day. I asked Ma Ponk about her and her health. Even though she was white, everyone in the black community knew her and of course the black maids and gardeners kept a constant flow of information coming.

"Miz Knight ain't well. Her sight is poor, but she still sewing. Antiseptic keeps her yard up and Ida still cooks for her. Now you go see her, 'cause she's all the time asking 'bout you. But I'm sho', Ida lets her know 'bout you."

I knew I would stop and see Mrs. Knight before I left Glen Allan. We passed by Hilton's food store where I had learned to sack groceries, cut meat, run the cash register, and be nice to customers. There was Mr. Hilton, and Mrs. Hilton still calling everybody "honey chile'," holding court, and paying homage to the upper class whites. As we drove through the town, we waved at people just milling on the sidewalk, sitting on the back of pick-up trucks, or standing in groups talking. They recognized the car, but stooped to see who this was in the front seat. With their hands over their eyes to give them better vision, they finally recognized me. I could see them laughing. I knew they must be saying, "Shoots, that Cliff in that car, Ma'y Esther's boy. You know he went north las' year."

Glen Allan looked the same as always. There were the quarters, the shotgun houses, the old folks sitting on the porch, but I would soon learn Glen Allan was changing. The revolution of the sixties was beginning to find its way down Number One Highway to invade the lifestyle that had prevailed since

Reconstruction. As we passed Allan Chapel AME, Ma Ponk very quietly said, "They been here, the Civil Rights folk. I didn't go, but somebody from up north came and talked at Allan Chapel."

Even though we were safe in the privacy of the car, Ma Ponk and Mama still spoke secretively, their voices low, as they talked about the Civil Rights movement.

"Brother Maxey knows 'em, and you know Jake, Miz Ayers' boy. He's al' time been looking out for us. But, son, God ain't 'sleep. No sir, in time He'll show His Self."

As we quitely talked about the Civil Rights movement and the pending integration of the schools, I looked back at Allan Chapel, just standing there. As a child I remember it as the place Mrs. Mary Maxey would have Christmas pageants. My Uncle Hurley, dressed as a shepherd in a multicolored bathrobe with a towel around his head, would sing "It Came Upon A Midnight Clear." During those few Christmas hours, our lives would be transformed and our minds and those of our parents would be transported to another time and place where hope for all mankind was born. And perhaps it was fitting that Allan Chapel take the lead in making that hope a reality in Glen Allan.

I would only be in Glen Allan for a few days and I had many people to visit. My mother always said I had the hot foot and couldn't be still. Perhaps she was right. Quickly I unpacked and hung up my clothes in Ma Ponk's extra bedroom. Then I gave her some money; I had saved up nearly fifty dollars for her. I knew to give Ma Ponk money, and that fifty dollars was good money, because my cousin Joe, Uncle Cleve's son, had once sent Ponk's sister Willie Mae fifty dollars. Willie Mae had told the whole community about that fifty dollars. Now I was satisfied that Ma Ponk could show Ma Mae her piece of money.

Ma Ponk and I talked for awhile, then I went over to my mother's house, where we unboxed the presents. "I know you are itching to visit everybody," my mother said as she admired the gifts I had brought for her and the children.

Within a short period of time, I began walking to the homes that I had known all my life to visit the people who knew me before I knew myself. I knew they would all have something for me to eat, and they would all want me to sit and talk for hours. I was one of their own, returning from up north.

I went to Buddy and Mary's (my mother's best friend), then to visit with Daddy Julius and Miss Ida. I tried not to miss any house or anybody.

Aunt Mary Ann and Miss Hester had passed on, but as I walked by their homes, I recalled the warm days when Aunt Mary Ann would invite me in for a cold slice of lemon pie made from scratch. Her house was always neat as a pin and her Frigidaire filled with goodies. She was Dr. Duke's cook and many times she'd repeat some of the Duke family's meals at her house. As I glanced at the once-regal house, slowly giving way to old age and the absence of its beloved tenant, I remembered the beautiful garden, the screened-in front porch, and the lady who cooked wonderfully and dressed in Sunday clothes even during the week. The porch had now begun to fall and the hedges were overgrown and the people living in Aunt Mary Ann's house seemed to have been totally unaware of the grand lady who once called it home.

Miss Hester's house had also succumbed to new residents. Young children now ran in and out of the house without regard for the garden that once grew prized roses. Mrs. Hester Rucker Jenkins was a mulatto. As I passed the house that once served as a model of pride, I laughed to remember those rare occasions when Miss Hester would invite us in and serve us big thick slices of angel food cake. She would always let us eat in her front room under the watchful eyes of the huge picture of her white father, sitting astride his horse.

Miss Hester was known as the Jewish cook, because all my life she had worked for the Freid family. There were only two Jewish families in Glen Allan and I'm told that the Freids were the more orthodox of the two. As little kids, we were allowed to pick up pecans in the Freids' yard, and if we were lucky and it was close to lunch time, Miss Hester would open the big kitchen window and provide us with delightful morsels of Jewish food. And the older Mrs. Fried was always kind as she spoke to us.

Continuing my walk brought floods of memories as I passed homes of family and friends. I even went into the famous juke joints to visit the owners I had known all my life. I stopped by Miss Phoebe's place because her daughter and I had attended high school together and her sister Minnie was my Uncle David's wife. Growing up in Glen Allan, I had never frequented the joints. Ma Ponk would not hear of it. But as a northern visitor, I was expected to pay my respects. From Miss Phoebe's to Miss Albee's place that was known as James Gatson's when I was a boy, I stopped and sat for a moment on the bar stools that had been forbidden territory during my youth.

As I sat on the worn red leatherette stools, I slowly turned and looked into the dance rooms where I had always suspected the best of times were to be had. Short order cooks were still taking orders for hamburgers and the Seeberg still held the top forty, but it was the magical dance room that really held my attention. James Gatson brought the best of the Delta blues to his place every Saturday night. Jax beer, Lucky Strikes, men with their hair pressed and waved, and lovely ladies who dared to dress invitingly would forget their week of farm labor as James' place transported them to a world of carnality all their own. I could still smell their Old Spice and Avon perfume as

I looked for the last time at the empty room that had mesmerized so many. As I said goodbye to Miss Albee, I thought about how, even in the midst of changes, some things remained the same.

The streets were still the same, several coats of deteriorating black tar and gravel, but they made me feel welcome nonetheless. I stopped and chatted for awhile with Mr. K. C. and a few of the men who were now involved in the Civil Rights movement. They talked proudly about Project Head Start, which was providing many Glen Allan blacks with their first chance at a decent wage. Robert Kennedy had visited Greenville, and his presence had acknowledged to the outside world for the first time the changes that were taking place in the Mississippi Delta. They were still Southerners, children of a segregated society, but they were men and women with great faith in the future. They continued to admonish me to do good, because I was their child, representing the entire Glen Allan community.

With their faith in the future ringing in my ears, I continued to walk and speak to everybody. One never came south to Glen Allan without appearing personally to sit on Cousin Beauty's front porch and enjoy a slice of candied sweet potato pie. Of course, I followed that tradition.

"Boy, now don't you forgit to go and see yo' Cousin Beauty," Ma Ponk had reminded me, "'cause if you don't, she'll be fussin' 'bout it and blaming me."

Not being one to cause verbal abuse for others, I intended to visit Beauty, assuring myself of a piece of her well-known potato pie. Her pies had always been the talk of the "Sisterworkers" rallies. Everyone had acknowledged her as the premier pie maker. No one knew her extra special ingredients, and she had never volunteered the secret. But all the "colored" women of Glen Allan knew that if Beauty made a potato pie, you could rest assured that the filling would be smooth and creamy and the crust light as a feather with the edges browned to perfection. As people ate and savored each slice, they could be heard to say, "Beauty done it again, she put her foot in that pie."

Of course, I was determined to have me a slice for old time's sake before I returned north. As I approached her house, built by my great-great uncle and Aunt Ester, I saw signs of progress. The once-plain house was now covered with siding and a screened-in porch had been added on the front. I knocked loudly, because she often spent time in the back yard.

"Cousin Beauty? You home?" I yelled as I walked around to the side of the house.

"Rest yo'self a minute," she called back. "I'm coming."

As I walked back to the front, I laughed to myself because I knew she had not recognized my voice. Maybe I was really becoming a Northerner. I stood on the front porch patiently waiting until I finally heard the front knob turn.

"Lawd, Cliff. Ponk told me you'd be coming. 'Course I know'd you'd stop here 'fore going back. Well, you looks good. Did you find ever'body all right?"

We continued to talk as I entered the familiar front hall with the twelve-foot ceiling. Her house was one of the four in Glen Allan built by the Peters brothers from Alabama. The Peters were black builders in the post-Civil War era, famous for the grand antebellum-style homes they had built for the white plantation owners. They had built their own homes and those of their sisters in a similar style, and these still stood in Glen Allan as testimony to the remarkable skills of the Peters. As we walked through the crowded hallway, we passed the locked room, which was her guest room and the place where the mysterious Miss Sue stayed.

Once, years before, I had merely glanced into the room and Beauty had matter-of-factly said, "Got to air it out. You know that was Sue's room." Even though Cousin Sue had her home in Glen Allan, she often left for months to visit New Orleans. Rumors were plentiful regarding those visits. Most folks said that quadroons and Delta mulattos were involved, but nobody openly discussed it.

Miss Sue's door, the hallway, and the big kitchen still looked the same. Cousin Beauty, called Black Beauty in her younger days, was old now, but still the prettiest black lady most of us had ever seen. She knew I'd come expecting sweet potato pie, and she wasn't about to disappoint me.

"Set down," she said, and I took my place at her kitchen table.

I could hardly wait. Cooked in her worn pie tin, the sweet potato pie gave off a heady aroma of fresh vanilla as she sliced me off a big piece. Then, as she reached to the top shelf of the china cupboard to get a Sunday saucer, I knew I was no longer just little Cliff. In that wonderful moment as she handed me my own slice of her famous sweet potato pie on her best china saucer, I knew I was an honored northern cousin who had come home.

As I filled my stomach with pie, Cousin Beauty and I filled an hour with conversation about Cousin Sue, Tootsie and St. Louis. At last, I realized that Ma Ponk would probably be standing on her front porch looking uptown and trying to figure out why it was taking me so long. I was Ma Ponk's boy, but I was also Glen Allan's son, and I still had people I wanted to see. I continued on my way, waving at Mr. and Mrs. Rainy, Miss Nute, as I walked uptown. I was headed now to see Mrs. Knight, the white lady whose leaves I had raked, the seamstress for the town of Glen Allan. Mrs. Knight was one of these white Southerners who had always made me feel warm and human, inviting me into her dining room to share lunch. Ma Ponk had insisted that I visit her, and of course I would.

In addition to sewing, Mrs. Knight had also sold used clothes, including those owned by her nephew, little John Boyd, a student at Ole Miss. She would always give me first pick before hanging John's clothes up for sale. I would later learn from another nephew of Mrs. Knight that he, too, wore little John's hand-me-downs. He assured me that neither one of us had the fun in those clothes that his cousin enjoyed while a student at Ole Miss.

We both knew the South was beginning to change, but neither Mrs. Knight nor I talked about voting rights or the integration of the schools. We just talked about her failing health and my progress. I left feeling it had been a good visit, not knowing at the time it would be my last with this kind lady who had given me so much encouragement in my youth.

I spent more time than I should have stopping, talking, and tasting at nearly every house along those familiar gravelled streets, but I had one more stop to make. I had saved the best for last — my visit to the house where I was born. This was my special time to see Poppa and his wife, Miss Sissy.

I couldn't wait to get to Poppa's house. I loved my great-grandfather, and his new wife Miss Sissy treated me warmly. Somehow Poppa's house didn't seem as big as it used to and the tall steps were easy to make. When I got there, Poppa was sitting on the front garret (as he called the porch), smoking his pipe, looking just like he always looked. As a respected preacher, Poppa always wore a suit, even when at home. Rocking in his chair, his head shiny and bald, he looked up from his reading and his old weather-worn black face became very bright as he called to his wife.

"Sissy, what you doing back there? Come on out here. Cliff's here from St. Louis."

Miss Sissy was as small as Poppa was big — very dainty with a syrupy voice that played to your feelings. I could hear her coming through the small bedroom.

"I'se coming Elder Young. Lawd, I'se so glad to see that boy. How long is he here for?" Wiping her hands on her white-turned-gray chef's apron, she opened the screen door and threw open her arms.

"Oh boy, you sho' look good. And I can tell you ain't been in the sun. You know I'se making a car'mel cake. Now set right here by your Poppa and let me git you a piece."

Hugging Miss Sissy, sitting by my Poppa, and eating a big piece of Mama Sissy's caramel cake was a true welcome home.

"Don't forget to visit yo' Aunt Mozella," Miss Sissy called as I left Poppa's house. When I said my goodbyes to Poppa, he seemed slower, and I realized for the first time that he was an old man.

In just over a year, the Glen Allan I knew was slowly but surely undergoing change. Though limited, the Civil Rights movement had begun to make a difference. People who had not voted before were talking about their rights. And as I spoke with Jake Ayers, Mr. Mapp, and some others, I learned that the way in which blacks and whites related to each other was soon to change, permanently altering the face of the segregated South that had been my home.

Not only was the structure of the society changing, but also the people themselves. Mr. and Mrs. Louis Field had moved away. And Uncle Abe's meticulously sculptured hedges were not as I remembered. Mrs. Florence's legs were giving her trouble. There had been a few deaths. Still, I was glad to be home. It was good to feel the connection between hearts.

Even though much was changing, many things remained the same. The people of Glen Allan were still kind and thoughtful, and at each house I was offered food and fruit jars of soda pop. St. Mark's Church was as fervent as ever, and the sermons just as athletic and full of fire as I remembered. Unlike St. Louis, here there were no chandeliers and the preacher's suit was shining from wear. But when the people began to sing the songs of their faith, there was little difference between the two congregations.

My mother prepared a big meal in my honor before it was time for my trip back to St. Louis. Smothered steak, rice, and banana pudding were part of a feast reserved for a northern guest — me.

I enjoyed my visit. Much of what I remembered about Glen Allan was still there, but I could feel changes coming. The old people had held up well, but it was now time for a new generation to set the pace for my hometown. I also knew it was time for me to return north. Glen Allan was not in my future, although it would always be in my heart.

"Don't be like them others and quit writing or visiting," Ma Ponk said as she gave me a small bag of pecans to take to Lucille.

I looked at her fragile body. For years Ma Ponk had taken care of our family and worried about those of us who lived north. She was getting older herself, but still seemed to be a tower of strength.

I took an early bus from Greenville so that I could get to St. Louis on a Sunday, making it easier for someone to pick me up at the bus station.

The bus ride back to St. Louis was just as tiring as the trip south had been. Ma Ponk was right, I reflected. A bus will pick up anybody who waves, and this one did.

But for some reason, the trip didn't seem as long.

St. Louis would be a welcome sight. I could hardly wait to get to the confectionery and my new friends. I felt like a Northerner. I guess Miss Sissy summed it up when she said, "Boy, the North 'grees wid you. You sho' looks good."

CHAPTER NINE

"Shet Up and March, Boy"

My first year in St. Louis was over. By mid-summer of 1964 I was beginning to realize that my dreams of job advancement and college education could be cut short any day by Uncle Sam. The war in Vietnam was real and the city was sending her sons and daughters. I knew that I could be drafted at any time, and I was afraid of the army and of being sent to the front lines in the jungles of southeast Asia.

I didn't share my fears with anyone, but service in the military began to look more and more like an inevitable part of my future as the war escalated. The only question remaining was whether I would go as a volunteer or as a draftee. I decided to exert as much control as possible over my life. I told myself I would visit an Air Force recruiting station, just to get some information. So, on a sultry St. Louis day in late July, I set out for a walk down Grand Avenue, a short walk that would change my life.

As I left the confectionery Aunt Clara called out, "Cliff if you going up to Grand, get me some deposit slips from the bank." Without much hesitation I replied, "Okay," and headed out the door, stopping to speak to Miss Missy who always sat outside sewing and altering our seconds into first-hand clothes.

Without thinking, I passed the bank and kept walking until I came to a familiar sign — a picture of Uncle Sam, dress hat and all, extending his boney fingers, and supposedly telling me that he wanted me. Within two hours, I had, without consultation of family or friends, joined the United States Air Force.

The word spread throughout my church community: "Cliff is leaving for the military." This was more than just enlisting, for we were by now watching death in Vietnam on the news nightly. Of course others had either been drafted or had enlisted before me, but, as all my friends came together to tell me goodbye, I was suddenly scared.

It was too late for me to back out. I informed my Mississippi family, gave notice at the bank, and prepared for my August seventeenth departure date. Within a few days, I changed uniforms. Leaving behind forever the messenger's cap and navy blue coat, I traded up for Air Force blue.

Preliminary physical completed, I was assigned an Air Force identification number. Prayers, friends' addresses, and promises to stay in touch became my choice possessions as I again packed and prepared to board a train into an unknown future. I said goodbye to Lively Stone, Jefferson Bank, and the confectionery. Carrying a minimum number of my belongings in a small leather bag, I joined the other guys on a blue bus which took us to the St. Louis Grand Central railroad station. From there we boarded the Lone Star south to Texas.

It was August 17, 1964, and I was starting another train ride, only this time there were no family members at the station and I had no packed lunch. Everything was different, but the feelings of fear and expectation were the same. The crowds of strangers scurried with their piles of luggage, while ordinary people stood in the waiting areas with wonder and excitement in their eyes watching their loved ones board and deboard the train.

As I walked with my group, I felt just as alone as I had two years earlier when I left my native Mississippi Delta for life north of the Mason-Dixon line. Once again I was faced with making new friends in a totally new world. I didn't need the assistance of the ever-present porters, but I still nervously glanced at them for reassuring smiles and directions. We had orders, instructions, and a senior recruit to manage our trip, yet my fear of the unknown was as real as it had been the year before. Now as then, there was no turning back. Without any fanfare, without tears, without familiar faces at the window, the group of us new recruits headed to the military and, perhaps, to war.

This time I wasn't asked to go to the colored coach. Black and white alike, we all sat together, our eyes filled with the kind of fear and expectation that knows no color lines. Jerry Williams, an eighteen-year- old white guy, and I were paired together. I had first met Jerry in St. Louis at the recruiter's office on the day we both enlisted. Our long monotonous train ride on the Texas Lone Star formed the basis for a friendship that would last through basic training.

The train hadn't changed in a year. The aisles were still small and the windows still gave us the chance to see the outside world pass silently by. Just as I had fifteen months earlier, I sat in my seat holding a brown bag tightly. It wasn't a bag of food packed with love and care this time, but a bag holding my military orders. I listened as Jerry bemoaned the fact of leaving his girl and the St. Louis Cardinals. Finally Jerry and I were both talked out. We settled back into the rather worn seats and silently listened as the train hummed along, loaded with passengers, young and old, of all descriptions. As I fully realized that I could not stop this southbound train, I began to accept the fact that my dreams of being a Northerner had been altered, perhaps forever.

I had always pictured my life to be just like my uncle William Henry's. I would go north, go to school, get a good job, and return home each summer for the rest of my life to let Poppa, Mama, and the rest of the family know that their son had made them proud. Now, with a little more than a year in the city, I found myself embarking on a career that had not been part of my childhood dreams.

Life as a soldier had never been my goal, but now it was becoming my reality. And as the train tracks led us into the night, all I could do was think of my grandfather, Daddy Julius back in Glen Allan, and all the men and boys of the town who had learned to hunt.

My cousins and friends had all learned from boyhood how to handle a rifle with the ease of the trained soldier. I recalled how Uncle Johnny and others had adapted to sharp shooting. Being younger, I would watch with wonder as they waged pennies to see who could shoot the most cans off the fence post and listen as Ma Ponk warned them not to hit her dog. They were all good, hardly ever missing a can. As the Lone Star guided us farther into the night, I could almost hear Daddy Julius getting the boys ready for the rabbit hunt in the woods behind Mr. Thomas's place.

Once the cotton had been picked and the weather turned

cool, there was little work left to do in the fields around Glen Allan. This became the time to go hunting, both for food and sport.

"Mack, where's Johnny?" Daddy Julius would call as he walked out of the house carrying his prized .22 over his shoulder. Dressed in blue overalls, wearing his ever-present hat, and chewing on a match stem, he was the leader of the hunt. When they heard his call, Johnny and all the rest gathered in the front yard where they began laughing and joking as they shared bullets, Lucky Strikes, and bits of chewing tobacco.

With Daddy Julius leading them, they all rallied together and headed down the gravel road to the back of Glen Allan where the woods were thick and there were plenty of rabbits. For the better part of the day we'd hear an occasional shot from the woods, until finally in the late afternoon the hunters would return home with scores of rabbits hung on their belts or in gunny sacks.

That night the smell of stewed rabbit with pepper gravy over rice would be coming from nearly every house in our little community, and the smell of gun cleaning oil mingled with the aroma on the night air. The hunt was over. The men were home. The rabbits had been cleaned, cooked, and served. All the guns were put away for the next hunt, which could come just about any day during the fall season.

The passengers of the train were quiet, but my memories were vivid. I could see the hunters of Glen Allan, their strides of confidence and the ease with which they handled their weapons. But I had never wanted to be a hunter; I'd always had other plans. I was going north where there weren't any fields and no rabbits to hunt. So I never became a part of the group who at early ages learned to shoot with comfort and skill, I never learned to break down the rifle clean it up real good, shoot a can off a post, or aim carefully at my dinner.

Now as I sat in the darkness with only the intermittent sounds of Jerry's snoring, I wished that I had learned to hunt. Here I was, off to war, without ever having killed a rabbit or shot a blackbird off a telephone pole. Things certainly hadn't worked out the way I planned. Soon I would be required to know how to shoot, not just for marksmanship, but maybe to save my life. Wondering about my life as a soldier and my future, I fell asleep and I would sleep soundly all the way to San Antonio.

As the Lone Star pulled into the San Antonio train station, I was almost as impressed as I had been by the St. Louis train station fifteen months before. It wasn't as big and crowded as St. Louis, but when I saw the number of young men and women gathered there with their small bags, I somehow felt that this particular train station had been waiting for me all my life. I had spent most of my life dreaming of trains and train stations, the vehicles to carry me to the North and the gateways to welcome me there. Even though San Antonio was off course, this was a train station nonetheless. I saw more Hispanic people than I'd ever seen before, but interspersed throughout the crowd there were men in blue uniforms who seemed to be in control of every move we recruits would make.

I had little time to take in this new world unfolding in front of me. It seemed we were only there for a moment when our leader connected with the blue bus that would take us to Lackland Air Force Base, my new home.

This bus ride served to introduce us to the mental attitude that would be necessary to survive in the military. The cordial tone of civilian voices was left behind at the train station, not to be heard again for many weeks. Each bus was managed by a sergeant who had practiced bully calls all his life. All the way from downtown San Antonio to Lackland Air Force Base, the sergeant shouted instructions at the busload of green recruits. Our initiation had begun. From now on, we'd learn to sit up, shut up, and listen up, no matter how unpleasant the tone of voice. I was reminded of Mississippi where I had first learned that it's best to be seen and not heard.

In St. Louis it had taken me weeks to begin to acquire the clothes, hairstyle, and speech of my new environment. The Air Force managed to change all that inside of a few hours. Upon arrival at Lackland we were herded into one large building which served as the entry point, where a complete transformation took place. We watched in awe as every minute saw the chipping away of a piece of our former selves. We went in with hair, we came out with no hair. We went in healthy, we prayed to come out healthy, after the rigors of a complete medical exam. We went in dressed to suit our own various tastes, we came out with a whole new set of clothes, a common blue uniform.

That first-day haircut might as well have been done by Mr. Will on his back porch in Glen Allan; the military barber whacked off all my tightly-curled strands that had just begun to take on a northern sheen. The process of being issued uniforms brought back to me vivid memories of Stein Mart on the Levee in Greenville, Mississippi.

Yearly, prior to the start of school, we'd find ourselves, along with our parents and every other child and parent from the farming community, racing through Stein Mart to get our school clothes for the fall. There was never enough money to buy anything other than bargain brands. We all rushed through the process of looking for blue jeans, plaid shirts, and shoes, hoping to find what we needed while there was still a selection. Under the watchful eye of the white sales matrons, our parents quickly, and without much measuring or trying on, eye-balled our bodies and purchased accordingly. Needless to say, eye-balled blue jeans never quite had the tailored fit.

They were good clothes, but most often too big for the intended wearer, a defect that was quickly handled by the saying, "You'll grow into them."

Once again, at Lackland, there was no time to measure and try on uniforms. As we paced our way down aisles and aisles of sameness, again under watchful eyes, I found myself quickly eye-balling clothes and moving out. True to form, just as in my formative years, the clothes didn't fit. This time, however, I was less than enthusiastic about growing into them. I almost cried as my black pointed-toe shoes and sharkskin pants were taken from me, to be returned home.

Outfitted with oversized clothes, shoes totally unfriendly to my feet, and caps and hats that moved with my head, I was now attired to answer my country's call.

Almost as quickly, Texas and the Air Force introduced me to a new language, which like the uniform was designed to make us homogeneous. It had taken me much practice with the aid of Mickey, Oscar, and my other city friends, but I had finally begun to pick up a slight "ring" to my speech. This much-prized ring would not serve me well in the Air Force, as I found my conversation relegated to "yes sir" and "no sir."

Thus, in record-breaking time, we were examined, proctology and all, our heads were shaved, we were provided clothes that didn't fit, and we were all given the same name — airman.

My new home was a far cry from the Mississippi Delta, but even farther from the North of my dreams. As my new friends and I began the process of settling into our new lifestyle, I realized that, more than my limited time in St. Louis, my former life in the Mississippi Delta had prepared me well for the rigors of military life. From the very first day at Lackland, my mind was overpowered with memories from my southern childhood.

Marching was a daily menu item. However, I was used to hot sun and walking. In boot camp I recalled with great clarity my days of chopping and picking cotton from mile-long cotton rows, rows that seemed to me to have no end. While we marched to the cadence of songs unfamiliar but soulful nonetheless, I remembered how, during the long hot days in the cotton fields, I used to dream of moving north. Now I dreamed again of a life less confining and more exciting. I dreamed of St. Louis and all my friends. I had barely gotten the chance to experience that life, and I longed to return to it. But first I would learn to march and shoot. I never learned to use a rifle with the grace and confidence of Daddy Julius and the rest of the men back home, but learning to march was easy. My feet remembered their cotton-row days and proceeded to march without me.

The sun was equally as hot in Texas as it had been in Mississippi, and the streets we marched were as long as those cotton rows. I found myself again under the watchful eye of the straw boss, only this time he was called the drill sergeant. The straw-boss' sole purpose had been to structure our lives to the will of the plantation owner. As we marched to the tune of his frown and chopped cotton to the cadence of his mostly angry voice, we silently worked to obtain his favor. Now, the straw boss wore a soldier's hat, dark glasses, starched khakis, and a black face. He had a voice that boomed orders from one end of the troops to the other, and I once again marched silently, careful not to anger the sergeant while trying to gain his favor.

The orders came fast and furious. We were given little time to analyze our state of being. I found myself forming a bond with my fellow recruits based on our determination to survive the drill sergeant's verbal abuse, his face so close to ours as he verbally abused us that we felt as if the two were one. It was partially that planned abuse that made us form a relation-ship based on a common goal rather than on our social differences.

Of course, I missed the city and all the sounds that had set it apart. I missed KATZ, and the Motown music Elder Scott had taken such great pains to warn us against. Motown sounds meant the city to me, but all I heard here in San Antonio were the country sound of pop tunes like "Pretty Woman."

At Lackland I experienced my first real encounter with integration — living next bunk to young men of different races, eating together in the mess hall, and facing a common enemy, the military lifestyle. Together we made our beds, only to have them unmade by our drill sergeant because they weren't made well enough. Together we climbed walls, crowded under barbed wire fences, and swung on ropes over man-made lakes. Green uniforms, short hair and a common treatment made us all alike, and all like them — military men. My best friend continued to be Jerry Williams, the white St. Louis "homeboy" who had enlisted in the Air Force the same day I did. At last I was finding what I'd dreamed of since Aunt Georgia invited me north where "My boys play with the white boys who live next door and they eat at each other's house."

Even though Glen Allan had provided her share of soldiers, I don't remember many "off to the military" celebrations. But the war in Vietnam would invade our small town, and Glen Allan would have far too many celebrations sending her sons and daughters off to the other side of the world, to another delta. Though an enlistee from Missouri, I was still a Mississippi boy. The people in Glen Allan, filled with hope and determination, admonished me in their letters to be like my cousin Joe who had enlisted in the Air Force out of high school.

According to Uncle Cleve and Ma Mae, his parents, Joe had "done real good," and his periodic returns to Glen Allan only served to verify their claim. Joe had decided to make the military his career choice and proceeded to improve himself in those activities that pointed him toward military success. Joe was a soldier, always looking crisp in his uniform even when home on leave. His picture was displayed with pride in Ma Mae's front room, and upon his return to Glen Allan, he would sleep in the comfort of the guest room that had always been reserved for the guest from the North. Joe had been to Europe, "overseas," as I recall his father proudly saying. "Overseas"; I figured that must qualify as north.

I was in Lackland the same as Joe had been, but I also recall seeing a framed sharp-shooter certificate hanging on his parents' wall. Joe knew how to shoot and hunt. Uncle Cleve had taught him. Except for a few unsuccessful times, my lessons were not that good. For some strange reason, I could never hold that rifle with the right poise. With the others, rifle, hand, and shoulder seemed to go together. Not with me. I was awkward and the gun would never cooperate.

In the military, days began to fade into weeks. After exhausting all of our efforts to convince the power structure that they'd be better off without us, we finally came to grips with our fate. We were airmen. Slowly but surely, we watched as our style of walk changed and listened as our diverse accents blended to become one voice, militarily controlled. The food, though cooked in bulk and still highly suspect, had begun to take on some respectability. Even the traditional mainstay had managed to gain a degree of favor. This was chipped beef in creme sauce over toast, which had come to be known as "S.O.S." by those of us not brave enough to speak the full title represented by that acronym. We marched daily into the mess hall, men and women of multiple races sitting and eating together, as I had watched people do in the big St. Louis cafeteria where I had first worked as a dishwasher.

Jerry, myself, and the others would eventually earn the privilege to visit town. By then we had bonded so well, we almost walked over each other as we trooped together through the downtown markets of San Antonio. Here we were completely immersed in Spanish, a language we could not speak and barely understood. Times of liberty would become more frequent as we neared the end of basic training, readying ourselves for technical training in Amarillo.

Once our commanding officers were sure that we had become part of their thinking, basic training was over and it was time for them to ship us off to technical school. It was special order AB-6363, issued 18 September 1964, that sent me and forty-five other men to the 3320th Technical School in Amarillo, Texas.

Amarillo was one of those places I'd never dreamed of visiting. Like many of my buddies, I had hoped to be sent somewhere more glamorous, but for now, we had our orders. Our names were alphabetically arranged and Amarillo was waiting.

Apparently, the Air Force was well stocked with blue buses, because when we got to the train station in Amarillo, we were ushered into yet another blue bus, complete with a new "straw boss" nearly as verbal as the drill sergeant we'd left behind at Lackland. Our new sergeant, like his San Antonio predecessor, issued us instructions as we were driven to the base.

Barren, barren, barren. I had never seen a landscape so empty of vegetation as the countryside I saw out that bus window as we pulled into the base. Just as we had feared, it looked to be the least exciting place on earth, but something about the wide-open landscape did provide a sense that the freedom we had all longed for during basic training might soon be found.

By the time we got to Amarillo we had bonded and our small group of guys had become friends. Jerry Williams was among those sent to Amarillo, and our friendship continued to grow as we began tech school and discussed the frightening possibility we might be sent to Vietnam. Though assigned to different barracks at Amarillo, we always spent our free time together, searching for whatever excitement this flat, dusty city had to offer.

All of us welcomed those new barracks at Amarillo. No more dormitory sleeping for us. We were given little rooms, with two iron cots, and we settled into them as gratefully as if they were rooms in a first-class hotel. Bill, my first roommate, was white. He was a big tall Southerner from Florida, and this living arrangement was definitely a first for both of us.

After days of training on computers, doing some limited marching, and speculations about our military future, we would quietly lie in our bunks and discuss the worlds from which we had come, worlds that were so very different from each other socially.

Bill and I weren't roommates long before he was transferred, but prior to his transfer, I remember a conversation that made us both realize just how separate our worlds had been.

As usual we had come in from school and supper, gotten cleaned up and prepared for bed. Lights were required to be out at a certain time, so when we weren't real sleepy, we'd just lie there in the darkness making small talk about an uncertain future. That night for some reason, we hadn't said that much and I was headed to sleep when Bill just started talking in the dark.

"Cliff, I know we are different and all, but I just got to ask you something."

I didn't know what Bill would ask, but I knew immediately that it would have to do with race. For a long moment, his words hung suspended in the darkness between our two small cots. There we both lay, wide awake but covered by the spell of night that had stripped away some of our inhibitions.

It was only moments later when he continued, but his pause seemed to me to last a lifetime. There was no need for me to say anything. I knew Bill would continue talking and I would listen.

"You ever made it with a white girl?"

The question was pregnant with history and social taboo. I could hear the tension in his voice as he asked me to share something deeply personal about myself. Out of the corner of my eye, I could see Bill's shadowed outline as he lay quietly on the cot with his arms under his head, his face to the ceiling. I propped up on one elbow and looked past him. The night and the darkness of the small room kept us from having to face each other. We both knew we could speak openly in the night the words we would never speak in tomorrow's morning light.

For a moment which encompassed my lifetime, I laughed to myself recalling my country rearing and the difficulties I had of really capturing the attention of the city girls I admired. I remembered Delores, Helen, Betty, Jean, and Ollie, all of whom had permanently slipped through my clumsy hands. Within another moment, I was laughing out loud.

"Man," I said, "I had to work hard just to get a date with one of my own, and you ask me about a white girl — and me being from Mississippi. You must be crazy!"

Back home in the Delta our schools weren't integrated and, except for rare working situations, we barely even encountered whites. I had no memory of even hearing a conversation about a social relationship between a black man and a white woman. That was a southern subject that had caused older blacks to strike quiet when we children would show up. The taboo was part of the gulf that had defined the historical relationship between black and white in my childhood world.

Even after I took the train north in order to experience the promised racial equality, I found a reality quite reminiscent of the South in this respect as well as in many others. Tonight in the quiet of our small military room, I was experiencing for the first time a conversation that went to the very core of our separate lives.

Bill didn't really respond to my words. I knew he had heard me, but for several long moments, only the silence answered. Finally, Bill continued talking, as if to the ceiling.

"It was like this where I came from: You weren't considered a man unless you had made it with a black girl."

We had both spoken our truths and they had become part of the night. We had been made roommates by a decision of others, but we had chosen to share our truths because we were friends. In an awkward way, we had tried to examine honestly the crux of our separate worlds, the taboo which had defined that division for centuries, and to find common ground. Not trying to answer each other, we spoke our truths to the night. Finally, as our words lingered in the darkness, we drifted off to sleep.

We trainees were a collection of diversity, from Stan Verroccio, the small Italian ladies' man, to my friend Jay Risher, the son of a military man, to Robert Canty, who dogged my every step and teased me unmercifully. We had all come from separate worlds to be a part of this one world. As we discussed the future together we all had a common wish that our new world would be better than the one our parents had known.

We had all labored under racial taboos most of our lives. Now even the historical terminology was being challenged. Words we had all used and heard all our lives, like "colored" and "Negro," were being supplanted by a new word, denoting a new racial pride. For the first time in my life, the term "black" was being promoted as the operative term to describe my race.

Basic training had been so intense that for a while the dynamics of the changes taking place in the civilian world had to take a back seat to a system that had for decades molded men and women from all backgrounds into a homogeneous military force. By the time we got to tech school, I began to realize that the military was accomplishing what I had only dreamed of in civilian life—integration. We were now being integrated into one Air Force squad.

Shortly after we arrived in Amarillo, our squadron commander chose individual squadron leaders from each barracks. Much to my surprise, I was chosen leader for mine. It became my job to march the men to breakfast, lunch and dinner, to make sure their rooms were cleaned and up to par for inspections, and to make sure everybody was present for squadron meetings. In short, I found myself in the role of a straw boss! I never really had a chance to become an overbearing straw boss, because the guys very quickly reminded me of just how temporary my position was.

Our group's nightly meetings were very different from the one-on-one "Listen up, Soldier" meetings we had had in basic training. I was responsible for making sure everyone was on time in the general recreation area for the meetings. We would assess the day and get further information from our commanding officers. Now that we were in tech school, we even had an opportunity to express our opinions. Of course they carried little weight, but we were at least allowed to say something. In these nightly meetings I realized more than ever the diversity of our backgrounds, but I also recognized how melded we had become.

Amarillo was military, but it was one small step toward the semi-independence we would all welcome when we were permanently assigned. Guys who had been rather quiet during basic training now began to open up, and strains of "flower children" protest songs could be heard coming faintly from behind closed doors.

As at Lackland, we all maintained our excitement over "free time" and our little group was determined to make the most of all that downtown Amarillo had to offer. Together we would listen to the voice of Roy Orbison singing "House of the Rising Sun," then roam the downtown streets looking for Amarillo's version of that House.

I survived my first months in the military, making friendships that would last for a lifetime. I washed dishes, pulled guard duty, went on liberty, completed tech school, and before long I was ready to take yet another train north to St. Louis. Here I would enjoy leave for a few days while awaiting my scheduled departure to Bangor, Maine, and my first assignment as an "automated supply specialist," managing inventory for the 397th Strategic Air Command.

UNITED STATES AIR FORCE

IN RECOG

AF FORM 1195 JAN 61

SMALL ARMS
MARKSMANSHIP

CERTIFICATE
OF ACHIEVEMENT

is presented to

MARKSMAN   CARBINE

TAULBERT CLIFTON

FOR QUALIFYING AS **USAF** MARKSMAN

JAMES L. ROSS, 2nd Lt., USAF
GROUND TRAINING OFFICER

DATE AWARDED 1 JUL 65

CHAPTER TEN

Miss Pinky's Soda Water Ice Cream

Nearing those last days of technical Air Force training in Amarillo, Texas, we all received our orders. Like most of the men in my company, I dreamed of an exotic assignment, but I would have no such luck. I got assigned to a base in Bangor, Maine—Dow Air Force Base. Maine was one of those states that meant very little to me, but I was quickly informed that Maine was just as cold as Mississippi had been hot. While many of my friends received the orders of their dreams, others were being sent to Vietnam. In light of Vietnam, the anticipated coldness of Maine seemed bearable.

As I spent my last day packing, it suddenly dawned on me that at least part of my childhood dreams had come true: I was again heading north. I wondered if I would now find a world like the one I had been told of when I was growing up. The heat of the Amarillo bunkhouse transported me back to those long, hot Delta summer days when we chopped cotton and dreamed of a better life.

It was always the hottest part of summer when we'd hire out to the plantation owners at a daily wage to chop weeds out of the cotton fields. Like the marching in boot camp, the chopping lasted all day. There, the drill sergeant was a straw boss and the mess hall was the cool side of Mr. Walter's field truck.

Most of us had started out before 5 a.m., had welcomed the early morning dew and greeted the hot southern sun. With each row of cotton chopped, it seemed as if the sun grew hotter, and the water boy lazier. Like a chorus of angels we would yell for the tired water boy from the first sight of the sun until we were sure that our day was almost done and we could soon expect the wave of the hat from the black straw boss signalling quitting time.

Long before noon our bodies were washed with sweat,

we had all chopped what seemed like miles of cotton rows, and the trees at the end of the cotton field (nature's toilet) seemed far away. We all looked forward anxiously to the lunch break.

Finally noon would arrive, and the lucky ones would find a shady spot under a big tree while the rest of us sat on the back of Mr. Walter's field truck. We ignored the heat and the flies as we kicked back with packed lunches of store-bought sardines, Moon pies, Showboat beans, and crackers.

Mr. Walter sold sandwiches directly from the cab of his truck, but Ma Ponk never did allow me the pleasure of buying them. She knew his captive audience would be overcharged and besides the food would be old—leftovers from his uptown juke joint and pool hall. Ma Ponk was determined never to be outmaneuvered, even by Mr. Walter.

Ma Ponk insisted that if you bought your lunch from Walter, you might as well chop for free. With him, you could charge at noon and he'd deduct at night. We only made three dollars per day, and, determined not to dip into that wage for food, Ma Ponk carefully and lovingly packed our lunch at home the night before. As a youth I wanted food from inside the cab, but Ma Ponk always won out. I joined the rest with my lunch from Ma Ponk's kitchen, and we'd wash it all down with one of Mr. Walter's cold Mr. Cola soda pops.

Ma Ponk would always try to find a cool spot out of the way, but I preferred sitting in closer so I could join in the conversations, or at least overhear last night's gossip. However, no matter where we sat, when the conversation turned north, Ma Ponk would join in. She was a seasoned traveller and quietly but firmly corrected those of us who had only dreamed of going north.

Many of those noon days were spent in the company of Miss Pinky and her pretty granddaughter, Betty. Miss Pinky, a heavy-set and light-skinned woman with blue eyes and white-folk hair, lived on our street and rode Mr. Walter's truck with us to chop cotton in the fields at the various plantations. She too had an opinion about the North because one or two of her daughters lived north and often times she'd go visit them. Most of us young dreamers would quietly listen as Miss Pinky weaved a world around her travels.

Miss Pinky always double-wrapped before going out in the fields, and wore her sun hat tied down with a large scarf. Her skin was nearly white, and she went through this painstaking exercise to keep her delicate complexion from the sun. Having no other choice than field work, many of the high yellow women of the South went to elaborate measures to preserve whatever status their light skin would bring. The extra wrapping of clothes was uncomfortable and many times would bring on spells of heat exhaustion, but it didn't matter. Double wrapping and extra-wide-brimmed straw hats were the acceptable dress for Miss Pinky and many like her.

Now, of course, Ma Ponk didn't double wrap, although she fancied her Jewish and Indian heritage. She would always say, "Pinky, gal, you git your color back ever' winter. It's too hot to wear all them clothes."

Although Ma Ponk and Miss Pinky were great friends, they always argued about their varying versions of northern life. On one particular day in July of 1961, I remember both ladies had completed a half day of work and were resting by the side of the truck, while the rest of us were talking north. Having finished her R.C. Cola, Ma Ponk started talking.

"Pinky, you gonna go see your daughter this year?"

"Well, Ponk, I'm not sure as of this moment, with Betty Jean working an' all, I'm jest not sure." Miss Pinky smacked her lips with a ring after each word.

"I might go to Highland Park to visit my boy," Ma Ponk said. "Are you going by train or bus, Pinky?"

"Not sure, Ponk, not sure," Miss Pinky answered rather quickly.

Later, Ma Ponk would lean over to me saying, "Pinky oughta be shame', putting on like that, 'sides trying to talk so proper and hide from the sun. She could jest come right out an' say she's going to ride the bus. That's how she went year 'fore last."

Ma Ponk, always trying to get the last jab in, assured Miss Pinky that she was going by train if she was going at all.

Meanwhile, the rest of us were again having our heads filled with the dream of going north. Ma Ponk talked about Highland Park, while Miss Pinky talked about Chicago and New York. As for us, we'd settle for any city just as long as it was north of Mississippi. While these two ladies talked, my mind was working overtime. Unlike me, Betty Jean had been north to visit with her mother, but she was a quiet girl, not given to much conversation. She'd usually sit with us and silently eat her lunch as the two older ladies went about their normal routine.

Our one-hour lunch seemed to come and go rather quickly. In spite of the heat and the hard work, we usually enjoyed the packed lunch or the over-priced food purchased from the cab of Mr. Walter's truck. All we needed now, everyone agreed, was an electric fan and a plump feathered bed, or better yet, ice cream.

With the mention of ice cream, Miss Pinky went into an enchanting conversation about how we could make the best ice cream in the world from cream-filled cookies and soda water. Of course, we had never seen her mix it, but she had us convinced that there was nothing creamier and colder than "soda water ice cream." She made it sound so good that the picture she painted would stay with us for the rest of the afternoon as we chopped our rows of cotton under the watchful eye of the straw boss and the Mississippi Delta sun.

For the rest of the day I mentally tasted the soda water ice cream that Miss Pinky promised, while also dreaming of living up north.

Now, with my bags packed to leave Texas on a north-bound train, I laughed to myself as the warm thoughts from the Mississippi Delta faded into the reality of the day. I had come to Texas on the Lone Star train and within hours, I would be leaving for St. Louis again to visit for a few days while en route to my new assignment in Maine. With only a few days to visit, I looked forward to seeing the familiar setting of the Spring Street confectionery, my St. Louis friends, and all the old customers that reminded me of my Delta relatives. My training was over, and I was ready to head north.

Even though I was excited that technical school was over, I realized that I'd also be leaving friends whom I might never see again. As we all gathered for the last time in the commons area and exchanged addresses, we laughed, but for some of us there were tears inside. The familiar barracks and the mess hall would soon be part of our history. As we waited for the bus to arrive, we watched young guys and girls fresh from basic training being unloaded. They would be the new residents in our old home and form memories of their own.

Finally our bus came, and without the usual military commands, we boarded for the short ride to downtown Amarillo where we would take the train to our various destinations. I wanted to go home. I could hardly wait to savor the smells, the taste, and the sounds of the city and my friends.

I arrived in St. Louis in my Air Force uniform, and as the train pulled in to the station, I looked out the window at the familiar scene. The porters were there, the crowd of people, and the station itself, still a grand lady and looking good. As I made my way outside to Market Street, I reminisced about my first arrival in St. Louis. It was threatening rain, however, so I quickly cut my day dreaming short, caught a cab and headed home toward Spring Avenue.

The cabbie talked about the war and questioned my assignment while bringing me up-to-date on the unrest still prevalent in the city. Even though I listened, my mind was racing up the stairs to my former room over the confectionery. As we sped down Market to Franklin and over to Grand, I noticed that much had changed. Even the driver of the cab wore a haircut style called the Afro, and his voice hinted of hurt, and of dreams unfulfilled. Nevertheless, with the surety of a seasoned cabbie, he got me to 2629 N. Spring Avenue just as the rain began to fall.

As we pulled in close to the curb, I nervously looked at the old store. Not much had changed. It was open and I could see the familiar outline of Aunt Clara as she waited on the customers. Aunt Clara and the others would be surprised to see me, but I just knew that they'd be delighted. The rain wasn't going to stop and I wanted in. I paid the driver, got my bags and made a dash to the door. As I quickly opened the familiar screen, I felt I was home.

Aunt Clara's surprise was more than I anticipated. While I was away, Spring Street had ceased to be my home. Aunt Clara tried to explain that "Brother" (Uncle Madison) had wanted to use the middle bedroom for something else. I stood there, stunned by the news. I listened, but I really couldn't believe what I was hearing. After all, I had enlisted from Spring. All my records indicated that 2629 N. Spring was my permanent address.

I was an adult now, but I felt like a lost child. I had no home and the rain was falling harder than ever. My first day home and I had no place to stay. As I sat in the room that had once been mine, I tried to think of an alternate plan. I needed a place to live for a few days before going to Maine.

As I sat there, still shocked, my mind fell on Oscar, one of my best friends. I decided to call his dad, Mr. Guyton, and ask his advice. As we talked and I related the surprising news, he listened. Then, without much hesitation, he invited me to come and spend those days at their home. He called me Son Taulbert, and I needed to hear that caring tone that day more than ever.

"Son, we ain't got much room, but you can stay with us and share the sleeping quarters with Junior and Eddie."

Assured that my presence would not dramatically change their lives, I quickly got the remainder of my things and waited for Oscar Jr. to pick me up.

The Guytons opened their hearts and their home to me. It was nothing new, for they had shared their space with southern relatives coming north for years. I was not a relative from their home town of Columbus, Mississippi, just a friend of their son and a member of their church. But their invitation could not have been warmer. Within hours, I had a new St. Louis address, 4000 Penrose, and this address would last me throughout my military career.

The generosity of the Guytons became more apparent when I realized that their sons would willingly let me share their rather small space, a tiny room at the end of a hall, just barely large enough for a bunk bed set. For the time period that I'd stay with them, Eddie, Oscar, Jr., and I would alternate from the bottom bunk to the couch. Even though we were crowded, we were family, and in the best tradition of the South, they had set a place for me in their lives.

My friends from Lively Stone Church and the Guyton family all made my days memorable, but somehow as I prepared to leave for Maine, I felt as if I were leaving St. Louis for good. All my life, I had wanted to find for myself the promised north spoken of by all those relatives who had gone before. I did like the city, but the military had interrupted my adoption process, and now I wondered if the streets of St. Louis would ever be my home.

The day for my departure arrived, and Oscar Jr. and many of my friends came to Lambert Field airport to see me off. It seemed like old times, because we all had spent many Sunday afternoons watching the planes take off and land. This day, many of the members of the choir were there to say goodbye as well. With this loving send-off, I boarded an airplane (for the first time in my life) and flew away to my future.

Arriving in Bangor, I hardly knew what to expect. All I knew was that this northeastern city had many years before served as a train stop for the underground railroad which took those earlier southern dreamers aboard to life north of the Mason - Dixon line.

Bangor in 1965 was not as large as I anticipated and it was quiet. The airport was small, and most of the people milling around were air force personnel. As I surveyed my new surroundings, there was little to remind me of St. Louis and even less of the hot Mississippi Delta.

There was no cotton, Mr. Walter's truck was thousands of miles away, the smell of sardines was nowhere to be found, and I was farther north than I had dreamed I would ever go. It was so far northeast, I was almost out of the United States. Even though the fall foliage proved to be a living watercolor, it was followed by piles and piles of snow, making me long for the weather of the South.

And so, part of my plans had come true, I had indeed come north! But none of it had turned out exactly as I had dreamed. Life in St. Louis had hardly happened before I found myself moving on to another city and a completely new way of life. My dreams of wearing a double-breasted suit, highly polished shoes, and talking like a Northerner had been put on hold. Air Force blues were the suit and "yes, sir / no, sir" were the major phrases of my conversation. I now watched the North from a distance, officially barred from most of the activities associated with civilian life.

The year 1966 found me staring out of a second story window of a green barracks, fighter planes stationed all around me, just looking west to nowhere. I was living near a town where my dark color was an oddity, where I found myself sharing my minority status with the Penobscot Indians, Bangor's true minority.

But here at Dow Field I found myself again living side by side with young men from nearly every ethnic group. My circle of friends included them all — a white Texan, a Chinese guy, a Jewish guy from New York, two black guys, one from Buffalo and the other one from Virginia. There were scores of others that I would get to know as we all daily watched the bulletin boards for orders to Vietnam. No longer bound together by our fear of the drill sergeant, we were now united by our fear of a war that could claim us at any time.

Even though we were in the military and especially concerned about Vietnam, we were still encouraged to go to college either on base or at the University Campus at Orono. For some of us, school became a means of escape from the thought of our potential involvement in the war.

Paul Demuniz, myself and a few others attended classes sponsored by the University of Maine and extension courses provided by the University of Maryland. Even though I was in the Air Force I felt good that at last I was in school. If all went well, most of my college education would be completed by the time my four years were up. Studying, watching the bulletin board, and enjoying the success of Motown and Aretha Franklin proved to be the medicine needed to calm our fears as we watched the turbulence of the inner cities and the horrors of the war.

Even though we had our daily routine of work, there were those moments when the fun of friendship was at its best. As a supply administrative specialist, I worked inside and concerned myself with the inventory of parts needed for the fighter planes, a job which introduced me to a white guy named Rice, a native of Maine.

Rice was different from most of the white guys I'd known before. I loved hearing him talk, pronounce car, park and just about anything with an "a" in it. But I recall our friendship not because of his eastern speech impediment, but because his mom would always send me thick crab salad sandwiches when he'd go home on the weekends. This was my first introduction to sea food. There, in the quietness of the hangars, we'd all sit and talk and laugh as Sgt. Brown ordered us around with no one really paying attention, and it all seemed better with crab salad on the side.

On those evenings when we weren't working or going to school, the base movie theater became our second home. While I was stationed in Maine, the motion picture industry introduced "Dr. Zhivago," one of the greatest love stories of all time. The characters of the movie, so intense and romantic, turned Dow Base theater into a house of tears as young men and women recalled the loves of their lives. As we all watched the coldness of the Russian snow and ice give way to the warmth of passion, we all truly believed that all we ever needed or wanted in life was love. For those few hours, we forgot the sounds of war and the cries from the inner cities — we were all Russians, in love, and determined to win.

The high of the movie lasted for only a while. Quickly we realized that we were not in Russia, but in Bangor at Dow Field with a job to do and a mission to accomplish.

Much of our day at work never really changed. So we spent time sharing our frustrations and dreams, and of course wondering why we were in the military and always questioning decisions of our commanding officers. The working area was tight, so we got to know our buddies pretty well. Even though we all had come from different Air Force commands, we had a common purpose. We had our metal desks and our swivel chairs and status boards to chart our activity.

Sometimes this closeness also brought out our personal biases. It was while in this close working environment with my friends that I observed the ill effects of bigotry from a different perspective. I watched a young Polish guy almost blow up because of the constant "Polish" jokes he was forced to listen to. Everyone was chatting about the weekend and complaining about the decisions made by the military brass, when all of a sudden, Rice made one of his thoughtless Polish jokes. Ski, a tall thin fellow, jumped up from his chair. His blood rushed to his face, his fists went up, and he was ready to fight. Sergeant Brown was quickly called to cool them off.

I sat at my desk and watched as the two white men gave vent to bigotry and anger, and I realized that people can hurt regardless of color. Even though the fight was averted, there was still tenseness in the air.

"We got a job to do," Sergeant Brown admonished them as we tried to restore some degree of normalcy.

"But, I didn't mean anything by it," Rice mumbled.

"That's what I've heard all my life," Ski replied as he, too, tried to get back to the routine. I was north now and in the military, but I was still seeing humans being human.

And our work was never really done, even though the F106 fighter planes needed parts and we had a real job to do. The First Sergeant still found it necessary to hold inspections. The news of a called inspection travelled fast, and as always, we weren't happy about it. As far as we were concerned, our barracks weren't designed to be our homes, so why pretend. But we had little choice, and the first shirt seemed to gain special joy from throwing in an inspection. We would get ready and, as always, be dressed and at attention at the required time. Three men living in one room found it difficult to divide the cleaning chores and turn the cinderblock room into a sparkling hotel suite . . . but we managed.

Robuck, my black roommate, and Kelly, the white guy, both Easterners, had little hands-on knowledge about cleaning. Our room was nondescript, with very few pieces of wooden furniture, but those that were there were expected to be highly polished. With little time, we accepted our assigned responsibilities and proceeded reluctantly to cleaning. But I had learned early on at the white Methodist Church in Glen Allan how to make dull tile shine and wooden pews burst with pride. Armed with this knowledge, I proceeded to polish the few wooden pieces with the same zeal that Miss Ida had taught me as a child. As I oiled my dust rag, I thought about the many

Saturdays Miss Ida, my step grandmother, had taken me with her to clean the white Methodist Church.

"Ponk, you gonna let the boy go wid me today?" Miss Ida would call out to Ma Ponk as she was getting ready to head uptown.

"I reckon so", Ma Ponk answered. She gave me my instructions, "Don't sass Ida."

Even though I didn't like the long walk, I looked forward to the money I would earn. As we headed uptown, we passed by St. Mark's Baptist Church where Miss Ida was on the Mothers Board and a very important member. But we were on our way to the white church to shine and polish it.

The white Methodist Church was a showplace for the Glen Allan white community, almost the first building seen when entering Glen Allan from Highway Number One. It was a rather long walk from the back of Glen Allan, past the other colored area, past uptown and past the lake houses, but Miss Ida managed to make it religiously.

As we passed by Miss Doll's house, Miss Ida always commented on the value of teaching the boy early to earn his way. Despite the constant stopping and talking Miss Ida did, we would eventually make it to the church.

Blacks were not part of worship services at the Methodist Church, and we'd only be allowed to visit at the back if the funeral of a prominent white was being held. As with most of the white homes, we didn't go through the front door but through a side door. Miss Ida knew where all the cleaning utensils were kept and proceeded to give me the oil and rags needed to shine the pews while she went about the heavy work. Miss Ida was determined to make the Methodist sanctuary shine, and she did.

Thinking about home and the people there kept me dusting too long at one spot. The guys had to snap me back to the real world of inspection. "Hey T, you in a daze or somthin'?" Robuck laughed as we all hurried to shine it up.

So, armed with my southern cleaning skills learned at the church and with the reluctant assistance of my roommates, we set out to add sparkle and luster to the place we now called home.

Although being in the military was by far a different lifestyle than I had ever known, it was here that I experienced my first hint of Aunt Georgia's promise — whites and blacks living and working together. Robuck and Kelly and I were vastly different from each other, but we forged a bond of friendship. Crowded into our small cinderblock room were three cultures, three diverse points of view. We were all human, however, and we all faced the same frightening prospects of war.

For some reason, I had managed to get the single bunk. Its only advantage was that it had a direct shot to the john which we shared with two other guys next door. Kelly and Robuck had the bunk beds located next to the door which meant they controlled the light switch. They also had direct access to the metal clothes closets. But I controlled the entry to the john.

I guarded my space with great tenacity, which was difficult to do whenever the room held more than three people, which it often did. I had not forgotten my drill sergeant, nor was I able to leave my southern heritage for discipline behind. I managed to keep both Kelly and Robuck in a state of "Why T". I demanded cleanliness of body and room, and many times they gave me neither. As Easterners, they both had a natural ability to close their minds to the demands of the barracks commander and pay no attention to me at all. They were very different from each other, yet very much alike. Robuck, tall, thin, and black, for some reason found it necessary to wear dark shades and a French beret at all times when permissible. Kelly, white and blonde, fancied himself the reincarnation of James Dean. He lived in the mirror, while Robuck immersed himself in smoking and listening to jazz.

From the start I knew the two were destined to be better friends than I. They had learned to chill out long before the phrase became known. I found myself still being an uptight Southerner. Even though we shared the same space, we did very little together socially. We had our own circles of special friends. Perhaps I did envy their camaraderie. That was especially true whenever I recalled one particular night, the night the lights went out in Georgia — or, rather, in Bangor, Maine.

Both Kelly and Robuck, in from a week of duty, had gotten dressed to go out and party. A night out in Bangor was limited at best, but if there are party bars to be found in town, the men and women of the military could certainly find them. We had very little to celebrate, but any excuse for a drinking party was considered legitimate, and so, my roommates were ready to party. Held back by my strict southern rearing and scared to death to drink, I just watched as the two young men headed downtown to Bangor to have fun.

As usual, Kelly had stood in the small mirror for hours, basking in his looks and getting blonde strands of hair all over the sink. Finding a woman and ignoring the war were his objectives. Tonight he and Robuck were going to hit the town. And as always, Robuck said, "Come on 'T', let yo' hair down! Let's get some Ripple, some women, and party." Kelly would echo these sentiments as they both lit their cigarettes and barrelled out the door to catch the happenings of Bangor before the town closed down.

The party must have been good because both Kelly and Robuck finally crawled in together, sick enough to die. Instead of women, they had found some bad (or too much) liquor, and I watched as my two friends shared the john, puking one after the other. In St. Louis, integration had been illusive but here tonight in the quietness of our cinderblock room, the three of us laughed in spite of the smell as the sounds of war took a back seat to a party gone awry.

The next morning, my clear conscience and their aching heads were awakened by the yells from next door.

"Who puked?" Don Yeagle yelled as he and his room-mate were the first to use the john. "You guys are like animals, this place smells like crap ... and we ain't gonna clean it up."

The sounds from Yeagle's mouth were always the same. He was our next door roommate, who fancied himself as somewhat of an Ohio intellect, but a good guy. His room was really like a pig pen, but he insisted on a clean john. After we acknowledged that our room caused the mess, I had to charge back at him.

"While you are so busy trying to find out who puked, why don't you unclog the shower? It's filled with strands of brown hair, not black tiny curls or Kelly's blonde hair. If the shower trap had been clean, maybe the puke would have drained."

Needless to say, we continued our argument. Finally, I cleaned the john, dressed, and we headed to breakfast. With the barracks behind us, we forgot the argument. While we ate the worst grits in the world, Robuck and Kelly tried to make their drunken night sound exciting and filled with fun.

Our mornings and evenings were fairly monotonous . . . get up, clean up, eat up, and work up. But the weekends were heaven sent — our freedom, as we called it. Some of us went skiing, while others went to the library or took short trips back home. John Palozzi, one of my friends, always went back home to Utica, New York, for weekends. I was just as happy as he was because he'd leave his white and red Chevy with me and his mom would send back sacks of deli sandwiches. The only drawback for me was that John had the habit of having fun at the expense of my name. Even today I'm still afraid to check into any hotel between Bangor, Maine, and Utica, New York.

And for those of us who didn't go home, we were all entertained by the "boys." The boys lived on the other end of the barracks, little Harlem it was called. Except for tall Fred Cowley, a white guy from Providence, Rhode Island, and a white guy called Radar, the "boys" were black, and their leader was Orell Clay. Orell, always impeccably dressed whether in civilian or military clothes, was the "good life" incarnate. With his smooth black skin and the whitest teeth I'd ever seen, he held court on Saturdays. Orell's was a barracks room during the week, but "Orell's Place" on the weekends. Here we welcomed the best in soul sounds while getting our hair cut by our home-grown barbers.

None of us liked to go to the military barber for a haircut. The military barber never cut our hair the way we wanted it, and he charged more for this disservice than we felt a haircut ought to cost. We flocked to Orell's to get both style and savings in a haircut, and with plenty of help from onlookers, we cut each others' hair, while Orell told us tales of his glamorous life in New York. He was a ladies man and there was no doubt about it. Even though we all had our stories to tell, none were ever as exciting as Orell's New York stories. He was the best at keeping our minds off the war and our hearts filled with laughter and hope.

These Saturday gatherings began in Orell's room and spilled out into the hall. He always had the latest Motown sounds on the stereo, and everyone came to Orell's to listen and talk. We sat on the bunks, and when the bunks were filled, we'd sit on the floor, on the dressers, or stick our heads in from the hall. We all wanted to be one of the boys. Orell would be laughing, dancing, and lying all at the same time, and we paid rapt attention to his every move. He was backed up by other guys who echoed his every word. Orell's roommate was Fred, a tall, skinny white guy. We all wondered how he stayed so white, living his life to the constant cadence of Aretha Franklin, Marvin Gaye, and likes of Orell Clay.

By this time I had fully adapted to the military lifestyle and even the work assignment had begun to take on a degree of conformity. There were few surprises, and as in any work environment, correct politics went a long way toward making me a success. I was pretty sure I didn't want to make the military my career, but I still pushed to climb the promotion ladder. One thing I did was participate in the "Big R" program, whereby suggestions for improvement were evaluated, used, and awarded if chosen. I also wrote for the Freedom Foundation. Both of these extra-curricular activities were instrumental in my being moved up to the position of Supply Liaison to the base commander.

The command headquarters was very different from F106ADC supply station where had I started out. At headquarters we had desks, charts, carpet, and "lifers." I think I was the only non-lifer in the office. They all seemed to have been working on their retirement for years, and they all dressed, walked, and talked with military crispness. No one played the role better than Sergeant Mack. He was short, smooth, and black, pressed and precise with teeth that were perfectly, militarily capped. Sergeant Mack set the tone for our office. He had a white counterpart, Sergeant Levecchi, who served as our intelligence factor. Levecchi knew it all — stocks, bonds, retirement, the national political scene. He fancied himself as part of some undefined aristocracy.

I found myself anchored between these two personalities who had nearly forty years of military service between them. Day after day they hummed their way into that certain future they called retirement. I watched them from my wooden desk, and learned how to conduct myself in an office environment from these pros, who seemed to have spent most of their adult lives keeping sharp for retirement.

Although clouds of Vietnam hung over our heads, our days of work were routine. "War readiness" was the order of the day and we ran the command center with that mandate. Dow Air Force Base housed strategic planners as well as fighter planes and trained pilots. I found myself charged with the task of coordinating the supply activity and making a summary report on the status of all parts ordered and the corresponding inventory. By mid-morning, my job would be complete, so I spent the afternoons studying for the classes I was taking at the University of Maine on the Orono Campus.

One of my English class assignments introduced me to Henry David Thoreau and *Walden Pond*. Fortunately for me this book was the favorite of the commander, a fact I learned one afternoon when he unexpectedly came through the office and caught me at my desk reading it. I braced myself for a reprimand but instead I got a verbal pat on the back. "Good material, soldier. Do you enjoy Thoreau? He has always intrigued me. His works are good for your mind."

I didn't have time to reply before the small man hurried on through the office. Even though he had the rank of base commander, he had never come across to me as the military bully. After that day I regarded him a little bit differently. His comments on Thoreau had given me a peek into his life outside the military. From then on, I saw him as a soldier on the outside only, wearing the right clothes and having the rank. Inside that uniform was a man who read Thoreau. *Walden Pond* and its philosophy did not make a significant impact upon me, but it was politically correct, at least on that base. And I think the base commander remembered that moment whenever he saw me again, for I was treated with a new respect. Henry David Thoreau had made my military life a bit easier.

Once the office routine was established, our work day never changed. We all did our jobs and looked forward to our exit dates, whether after four years or twenty. Within our established routine we lived for the weekend and critiqued the "brass" during the week. There was only one day that stands out in my memory as different. That was the day of the mock war.

All the commanders received word that a drill was imminent and the entire base should be in a state of war readiness. This obviously affected every airman, including me. The Vietnam War was now at its height, and everybody took this war readiness drill seriously. As soon as it was announced, we were issued gas masks and instructed in how to use them. We were told that the entire base would be fogged in with synthetic fog and that we would be required to don our gas masks and get from our barracks to our stations to take care of our duties. There was one element of surprise; we had no idea what time the foghorn would go off.

The announcement of the war readiness drill brought an element of confusion and fear to this base where most of the personnel had never experienced a real war. It was to be command-wide, with even the brass and the pilots (our prima donnas) participating. As we read the bulletins and listened intently to the messages coming over the base speaker system, we all wondered if we were being told the whole story. Even the lifers didn't trust a military maneuver that interrupted the established routine. And those of us who had reluctantly enlisted tended to question every act that seemed too military.

My co-workers and I readied ourselves to answer every supply material call. That night in our barracks, my room-mates and I speculated about the real reasons behind the drill as we waited for the foghorn to sound, beginning the drill.

"They're going to totally fog the base, and we can't use any lights. How do they expect us to get ready and move out without lights?"

"It's all going to be timed. We gotta get to our posts wearing those gas masks, dark or no dark, fog or no fog."

"There'll be fog."

We couldn't sleep that night, and our little cinderblock room seemed even more crowded than usual as we took short cat-naps and waited for the foghorn. Finally it came.

Stumbling over each other, we struggled into our gas masks and found our way down a tiled hall to the outside stairs. We felt our way through the man-made fog, and searched in the inky dark for our battle stations. Many long, tense hours later, daylight came upon us, penetrating the fog. We could see again, and the mock battle had been won.

By the end of the day our points for completion had been assigned and our routine was firmly in place. The fighter planes were back in their hangars and the pilots were at the officers' club. My one big moment had come and gone. This one-day drill of a fake war was the closest I ever came to being a military hero.

Our routine days turned into routine weeks and months as we paced ourselves, watching a war from the distance. The news media brought both the war and the unrest of the sixties into our barracks. I had come a long way from the Mississippi Delta. I had played war games with young men from diverse backgrounds and found some of the opportunity I had dreamed of as a child working the cotton fields of the South. Many of my friends, affected by the flower children, the age of philosophy and free love, opposed the war. But I saw the military from the perspective of my segregated upbringing, and it seemed radical enough for me. After all, it had been in the military that I had finally come face to face with men and women from different backgrounds. In the military I found integration, not as Aunt Georgia had promised, but at least here blacks and whites were yelled at equally. We were all thrown together and expected to get along, northern blacks who viewed their southern cousins with suspicion, white guys who found themselves using the same johns as blacks for the first time, and me, a Mississippi Delta colored boy trying to be a soldier a long way from home.

My dreams of life north of the Mason-Dixon line had been much better when I was chopping cotton at Hampton, Wildwood and Marathon plantations. There I could make the promises of the northern visitors be all I wanted them to be. There I could envision myself as always dressed as well as Uncle William Henry or cousin Earl from Detroit. Those days were gone, and now I knew the truth. Reality is never exactly as we dream it will be. Northern life had turned out to be much like Miss Pinky's soda water ice cream. While the sun was hot, her verbal mixture sounded cool and refreshing, and the more she stirred and mixed with her words, the more we savored the fantasy. But she and Betty never told us how her soda water ice cream turned out when they really tried to make it.

CHAPTER ELEVEN

Poppa: Breaking the Bread of Life

By the fall of 1965 I had travelled north to St. Louis, enlisted in the Air Force, seen the sights of Texas, and wintered in Maine. There, I, a black Southerner from the Mississippi Delta, had learned to snow ski, used the central library, and attended classes on the campus at Orono. I had quickly learned that the Dow Air Force Base mess hall cooks had no idea how to cook grits.

With perhaps a year of my Maine assignment left, I was at last beginning to feel as if I understood the Northeast. I had gotten used to the stares from Bangor youths, many of whom had never seen a black American as dark as myself.

I had also changed the course of the lives of at least one family in Maine as a result of having the blood type that an older white lady needed. Her husband later called to thank me, and added rather quietly, "I didn't realize that you all had the same blood as us."

The streets of Bangor had become as familiar as the

sidewalks on the base. I had made friends in the city and had a fair number of buddies on base. Still, I cherished those letters and phone calls from home. Using the phone to make and receive calls required no strategic skills in civilian life. On a military base thousands of miles from home, with only one phone for at least fifty men to use, calling home was tricky. Even so, our barracks' phone was our outlet to the world of family and friends left behind, as well as our instant contact to the late-night relationships established while we were out on the town.

Fortunately, the room I shared with Robuck and Kelly was close to the phone. This proximity provided us with instant access to news of the joys, sorrows, or triumphs of our friends. From dates being made or dates being broken to the call to come in and work overtime, the phone was a vital link. Most of my calls were related to work or the courses I was taking at the University. I seldom received a call from home, but was overjoyed when I did.

One fall night the phone rang outside my barracks door. For some reason, I let it ring. Finally someone picked it up and yelled out for me. Surprised, I jumped up and stuck my head out of the door.

"Hey man, you got a long distance one here," a buddy of mine told me.

Long distance, I thought to myself as I thanked the

airman and proceeded to take the phone. It was my mother. Her voice did not sound upbeat and happy. Very quickly she relayed to me the news that caused my heart to cry: Poppa had died.

Mama didn't say much. She just gave me the date and time of the funeral and told me she'd like me to come home if I could. I sadly said goodbye and slowly hung up the phone. I was stunned. Poppa was dead.

Kelly and Robuck were not in the room. I sat there trying to figure out if I should ask for an emergency leave. Then, as I sat alone in the quiet cinderblock room, memories of all the good times that Poppa had given me came flooding back, and I started to cry. Of course, Poppa was an old man and he had sugar. He would never eat right, but still I always figured he'd live forever. He was proud of me and I of him. I was Elder Young's great-grandson; this had always been a very important part of my identity. He was supposed to live in Glen Allan always so that I could come from up North and visit him. Now, I would never be able to visit Poppa at the big house again.

I laughed through tears as I recalled his holiday tradition of making cheap egg nog. Year after year I had been on hand to watch him put the raw eggs in the mixture, and sprinkle the cinnamon. I got to be his taster. He had made ordinary peppermint sticks seem more precious than expensive chocolates. And he laughed heartily every year as each of us gave him our expressions of love — big white handkerchiefs. I remembered Poppa's loving black face and bald head, his ever-present pipe, filled with the best tobacco that Prince Albert made. It took Poppa to make our Christmas holidays complete. But he had died, that's what Mama had just said, Poppa was dead.

When I was a little kid, and his wife Miss Sissy couldn't go, Poppa would load me up in his car and take me with him to some of his many revivals. Poppa was Elder Young, a well-known Baptist preacher. Tonight, as a grown man in far-off Maine, I just sat in the darkness re-living those special moments.

"Boy, let's hurry, can't be late for church," Poppa would call out as he headed out the front door to the car. "Yes sir," I replied excitedly as I put the last bit of grease on my face and knees. For some reason shiny knees were important for a colored boy. I always had to look right on those special nights when Poppa took me with him to the church where he was holding one of his yearly revivals.

We often went places together on the weekends, like Greenville, or Hollandale, Mississippi, but those revival trips were by far the most exciting. I could still picture Poppa, dressed and filling the pulpit, leading the congregation in song. Poppa was a good preacher and everybody said so. He would stand behind the altar, glasses and Bible in hand, looking out across the congregation with a sure sense of authority. And the people would almost always respond with fervor and respect. "Breaking the bread of life," as he called his scripture reading, was done with great religious pomp and circumstance. Whether his words were pronounced correctly or not, the tone of his voice held the church in awe.

My mind went back to one particular night at the small plantation Baptist Church. Though many of the church people worked in the fields during the day, they nevertheless arrived at the little church early in order to get a good seat. Poppa had a preaching reputation and with such a reputation came the supportive crowd. The deacons were there, though many of them had worked long, hard hours that day chopping cotton. The majority of the church leaders were women who occupied their seats in the area designated for them. They served as Mothers of the church, ushers, or had other assigned responsibilities. This little wood frame building, without the benefit of modern accommodations, located on the edge of a cotton field, now came to life, filled to capacity with wearied bodies and souls soon to be uplifted, as church began to happen.

Sinners were paraded to the front and the mourners' bench was there to accommodate their public confession of sin. Poppa would place me in the corner of the church directly opposite the area designated for the Mother Board and there

I would quietly sit and watch while the dynamics of worship transformed this small gathering of field hands into an ecstatic crowd of worshippers. For some, singing soon gave way to tears and outbursts of joy and surrender. I watched wide-eyed as the beat of the old piano, the timing of hand clapping, and rhythm of feet stomping created a musical environment all its own. The worshippers were expressing their faith while warming up the church for Poppa, who without a doubt was the star attraction.

As the old wooden building rocked back and forth, stirring up dirt from the wood-plank floor, I saw my Poppa come to the pulpit. Somberly dressed in his black revival suit, white shirt and tie, Poppa lifted his voice to sing. He seemed to have forgotten his hard day of work and the day he would face tomorrow. It was time for revival, he was the speaker, and saving souls took precedence.

He raised his hands to slow down the beat of the singing. The church, now fully engaged, slowed down at his command and shifted gears to sing with Poppa as he led them in a thought-provoking song, a Doctor Watts hymn. Tradition was behind him as he led the church in singing his revival favorite, "The Evening Sun Is Sinking Fast." And no one could sing that song any better than Poppa. Sung to Baptist perfection, it set the tone for allegorical comparison, letting the sinners know that their time was running out. I would stay awake as long as I could, listening and watching as Poppa talked about a better life in a different world.

Now, sitting in the darkness of the barracks with my mind in a small Delta plantation church, I thought about the better life Poppa promised and the dreams that I believed to be reality north of the Mason-Dixon line. It was at Poppa's house in the Delta where I had seen the best of the North, the well dressed men and women, kin and friends coming home, paying homage to Elder Young. I had heard all their tales. I had seen their stylish cars and dress. I had heard their proper speaking. I wanted more than anything to become a Northerner and return home to see Poppa and the family.

I was north now, I thought to myself, farther north and east than I had dreamed I'd be, in a place that was colder than I ever imagined a place could be. It wasn't cold tonight, just lonely, a loneliness filled by memories that would live forever. Poppa, my black Buddha of the South, had died. The world of my youth was slowly passing from my life. More than anything I wanted to return home to see them put Poppa away, but I feared I wouldn't be able to go.

I spent the next few days crying on the inside as I thought about the funeral. After discussing the matter with the commanding officer and checking the cost of a flight home, I finally came to the conclusion that I would be unable to attend. The family would probably all be home. Uncle William Henry,

Poppa's boy, and Poppa's sister, Aunt Georgia, and as always, cousins I didn't know. It would be a big funeral. Maybe the whole town would come out to see his last remains and mourn with the family over its loss.

As I shared the news of Poppa's death with Paul Demuniz and the other airmen that I had come to call friends, I remembered the joy of his life and the undisputed seat of power he held within the family. Poppa had made our world safe. He never possessed much materially, yet he had managed to instill within those who would listen a real sense of worth. In everything he did, from getting the smokehouse ready for the carving of the pork, to operating his small grocery store, Poppa — Elder Young — had stood out in the community.

Not only did he make Christmas the best of holidays, but he made every dinner a special time. Nothing was better than to sit with him on the sun porch where we ate during the hot summer months. I remembered jelly cake, sliced to perfection, and fried corn covered with fat back grease. Poppa would sit at the head of the table and pray — longer than required, I was sure — and eventually we would start our meal, always laughing, talking while we ate, and discussing the future. But now as I thought about him, laid out and fully dressed, I realized that the sun of our relationship which had shone so brightly had finally set. Poppa's favorite song, "The Evening Sun is Sinking Fast," had become his reality. He had been a bright spot in my life, but his sun had set, and now his life would become my treasure of memories, to carry with me in all the uncertain times to come.

Not only had Poppa died, but many of the other older residents of Glen Allan had seen their evening suns set. Still, I could not bury their memories. And as I continued my duty at Dow AFB while awaiting my new assignment, I spent many a cold, snowy night telling Paul and any of the guys who would listen about the Mississippi Delta, the place and the people I called home.

We talked about them all, Poppa and his '49 Buick, Ma Ponk, Miss Hester, Mr. Louis Fields, Mama Pearl, Aunt Lurlean, Daddy Julius, Glen Allan, the cotton gin, and all the small plantations that were located around my little Mississippi Delta town. The more I talked, the more I remembered. I realized that much of what I had dreamed and lived for had to do with people back home who had entrusted me with their dreams. They had never had the opportunity to make these dreams come true themselves, so they sent me north to find that opportunity. Now, in countless loving memories, they also brought me home.

Paul, Don Yeagle, Robuck, and others listened patiently as I shared my memories with them. Every evening they travelled with me to Glen Allan and were introduced to a new resident each time, people who lived their lives behind the wall of segregation and endured the pain of racism, but loved and nurtured as a matter of course.

"Cliff, you ought to write these stories down," Paul said one night. "Your stories are great. You make me feel like I know those people." But I wondered who would care about these ordinary "colored" folks. Still, I told my stories. Memories of the people from my home town and the troubles they had endured, and the good days of fun and laughter strengthened me as I anxiously watched the war escalate. I was afraid of the war, but I knew that if assigned to Vietnam, I would have no choice but to go. With this fear in my heart, writing my memories down began to seem important. The only life I had really lived was in the South, where, in both the best and worst of times, the best people in the world had loved me.

True, I had been born into a segregated world that had predetermined my social status before my birth, a world where my color would dictate my mobility. However, it was in the midst of that reality that I experienced the love and nurturing that would impact me for the rest of my life. In Glen Allan my people taught me the value of family.

Maybe the guys were right. The stories of these ordinary people would be worth writing down. So with pen and paper in hand and the sound of war in the distance, I started writing about those wonderful "colored" people, as I called them, who lived in the Mississippi Delta.

Both Poppa and Mama Pearl now were dead, Uncle Abe Brown was also gone as well as Miss Hester. Many of the people of Glen Allan were only memories, but as I sat in the coldness of the barracks the memories of their laughter, their scolding, their dreams for my life brought a warmth, a warmth I wanted to share. It was because of their faith in me that I had taken the train to St. Louis. Determined to make them proud, determined to be accountable for their investment of caring, I'd boarded the Illinois Central north from the Mississippi Delta. Still uncertain of my future, I was confident in the family I had left behind.

And so I began writing. Taking advantage of the free time I had in Maine, I began to write about a town that very few people knew existed, and about the people who lived there. Their memories filled pages and pages of notebook paper and writing about them kept me busy and helped keep my mind off the war, violence, and student unrest that now raged in the world around me.

The realities of the war were coming home daily. Friends I had made in the military were dying, and here in the USA, the large urban cities were under siege. A somewhat confused Southerner, I watched as we fought to free the South Vietnamese while the youth of our cities were marching for freedom. The North that I had dreamed about was virtually up in smoke. The cities that Poppa, Ma Ponk, and Miss Pinky carried as treasures in their bosoms were now tarnished with smoke from the fires and their luster lost to the reality of promises not coming true.

During those days scores and scores of my friends found themselves being assigned to duty in Vietnam. Because of my classification, I looked daily for my assignment notification.

Then one day my good friend Paul Demuniz received notice that he was being shipped to Vietnam. This was especially difficult, because Paul and I had grown close during our Maine assignment. We had taken college classes together. On those cold winter nights in Maine, we had shared our lives, told our stories and bonded.

Paul and his roommate Tom had taught me how to ski. Coming from the deep South, I knew hardly anything about snow and related activities. But that didn't seem to bother them. They dressed me in Paul's ski clothes, piled me into Don Yeagle's car, and we headed northeast to Sugar Loaf where I learned to ignore the freezing cold and accept the challenge of the mountains. In all the stories I'd heard from the folks in Glen Allan about our kin, I'd never heard of any blood relative who'd ever been skiing. Warmly dressed in Paul's clothes, with my rented boots, I set out to make family history.

Paul and I had made wonderful memories, and we pledged to always be friends. When I heard about Paul being shipped to Vietnam, I decided to take advantage of a special assignment notification for the 89th Presidential Wing in Washington, D.C. Realizing I had nothing to lose, I applied, along with thousands of others. It seemed like a miracle when I was chosen. Elated and overjoyed, I began to prepare myself for my new assignment. I knew I had been incredibly lucky in assignments, and I made haste to comply with all the requirements. I wanted to be ready for life in the nation's capitol.

Even as I prepared to leave, I realized I had come to like Bangor. It was so different from Mississippi, yet not very different at all. I appreciated the role that Bangor had played in getting the escaped slaves to Canada, but I also realized that over the years, the relationships between people of color had not yet matured. Perhaps this was because there weren't many blacks in Bangor, and those that lived there were very light in color. Still, even though my dark skin made me an oddity, I had never felt alienated here. I made friends within the Bangor community and formed relationships which could last a lifetime. And as I anticipated leaving for my new assignment, I realized that again I would be leaving good friends behind.

Now it was time to move on. As I prepared for my change in assignment, I was loaded with paperwork to complete. My friends kept chiding me, trying to figure out how I missed Vietnam. Without question I had received a good assignment. I had never been to Washington, but I had always wanted to see the capitol and the life that existed in one of the world's most important cities.

Anticipation mounted as I contemplated the future. After many extension courses from the University of Maryland, I would now have the opportunity to take classes on the College Park Campus. The 1968 presidential races had begun with candidates staking their positions. Even though John Kennedy had been assassinated, the foundations of Camelot were still there, and many of us looked to Robert Kennedy to rebuild the walls.

So much was happening all around me as I envisioned military life in the 89th Presidential Wing. But reality surrounded my joy as I watched a nation torn over the escalating Vietnam War. College students, the poor, and the disenchanted black urban dwellers were making their hearts known, and the media carried their stories. Dr. Martin Luther King had targeted our capitol as the focal point to prick the conscience of a nation regarding the needs of those less fortunate. This was the Washington I would face as I left behind the relatively quiet life I had found in this small corner of the Northeast, Bangor, Maine.

Finally the day arrived for my departure. Sad, but excited, I could hardly wait to get to the small airport in Bangor. After saying all the customary goodbyes, and accepting a generous dose of sage advice from my single friends, it was time to leave. As we walked out of the green barracks, I took my last look at the mess hall where they'd never learned how to cook grits. I silently said goodbye to the base which had served as my home and to the men and women who had become my friends.

Suddenly, I was reminded of that day almost five years before, when I left Mississippi with much anticipation to find my new northern life. Bangor's airport was hardly bigger than Greenville's train station. As I unloaded the car, I realized that I was alone again heading into a new future. There was no reason to cry, because I was grown up now, but I knew I'd miss my friends. Now I was surrounded by other airmen whom I didn't know and a few civilians departing on short trips. There was nobody here to see me off.

How things had changed since that last train north from Mississippi. Poppa was dead, and the train no longer ran to the Delta. Without a packed lunch or the advice from Ma Ponk, I knew I was completely on my own. But I had my orders and my new assignment.

I boarded the plane just as the sun was setting in Bangor. As I sat strapped in my seat, I felt excitement and perhaps a touch of fear. The engines roared, we soared into the sky, and soon Bangor was nothing more than a speck, much like the disappearing cotton rows I had left behind five years earlier. The higher we flew the smaller the speck became. We were on our way. Again, I sat and looked out the small window, not at cotton, but the billowing clouds that were slowly turning gray in the dusk. As we passed through the clouds, a rush of memories carried me from cotton fields to train stations to military barracks. For almost five years I had been travelling on trains and busses and airplanes. Tonight I found myself still travelling to the rest of my life.

Washington challenged me, but I knew I would make new friends, just as I had done in St. Louis, and Texas, and at Dow Field. I would cherish those relationships. The people I had met in my travels — Mickey Piggs, Mama Bulah, Uncle Madison, Oscar Guyton Junior and Senior, Jerry Williams, Paul Demuniz and all the others had found a place in my heart beside the ordinary people back home in the Mississippi Delta, the ones who never left Washington County, but sent their dreams packing with me and the thousands of others who had left before me.

I thought about them all, as my plane sailed into the night. Even in a world where passenger trains no longer served the Mississippi Delta to carry our dreams, there were those special people who watched over our lives from their front garrets, whose values didn't change, and to whom I still was accountable. For them family, friends, and community were still everything, and it was their unchanging friendship that warmed my heart. My memories of them would hold me steady in a changing world. They had personally wrapped their arms around me when I boarded the last train north from the Delta. Now I knew they had given me so much more; they had given me their vision of a land of freedom and opportunity, and the resiliency to see it happen. I felt their strength and knew that I would always be their son, as once again I travelled in search of our dreams.

The

Trustees and Officers

of

Freedoms Foundation at Valley Forge

announce with pleasure

the selection of

AIC Clifton L. Taulbert, USAF

by the distinguished National & School Awards Jury

to receive

The George Washington Honor Medal Award

for

"Defending Freedom Safeguards Amer⁺

1966

An outstanding accomplishme

helping to achieve a better understa

of the American Way of Life

Kenneth D. Wel
President

ment will be made on February 22n

FOR THE BEST IN PAPERBACKS, LOOK FOR THE

In every corner of the world, on every subject under the sun, Penguin represents quality and variety—the very best in publishing today.

For complete information about books available from Penguin—including Pelicans, Puffins, Peregrines, and Penguin Classics—and how to order them, write to us at the appropriate address below. Please note that for copyright reasons the selection of books varies from country to country.

In the United Kingdom: For a complete list of books available from Penguin in the U.K., please write to *Dept E.P., Penguin Books Ltd, Harmondsworth, Middlesex, UB7 0DA*.

In the United States: For a complete list of books available from Penguin in the U.S., please write to *Consumer Sales, Penguin USA, P.O. Box 999—Dept. 17109, Bergenfield, New Jersey 07621-0120*. Visa and MasterCard holders call 1-800-253-6476 to order all Penguin titles.

In Canada: For a complete list of books available from Penguin in Canada, please write to *Penguin Books Canada Ltd, 10 Alcorn Avenue, Suite 300, Toronto, Ontario, Canada M4V 3B2*.

In Australia: For a complete list of books available from Penguin in Australia, please write to the *Marketing Department, Penguin Books Ltd, P.O. Box 257, Ringwood, Victoria 3134*.

In New Zealand: For a complete list of books available from Penguin in New Zealand, please write to the *Marketing Department, Penguin Books (NZ) Ltd, Private Bag, Takapuna, Auckland 9*.

In India: For a complete list of books available from Penguin, please write to *Penguin Overseas Ltd, 706 Eros Apartments, 56 Nehru Place, New Delhi, 110019*.

In Holland: For a complete list of books available from Penguin in Holland, please write to *Penguin Books Nederland B.V., Postbus 195, NL-1380AD Weesp, Netherlands*.

In Germany: For a complete list of books available from Penguin, please write to *Penguin Books Ltd, Friedrichstrasse 10-12, D-6000 Frankfurt Main 1, Federal Republic of Germany*.

In Spain: For a complete list of books available from Penguin in Spain, please write to *Longman, Penguin España, Calle San Nicolas 15, E-28013 Madrid, Spain*.

In Japan: For a complete list of books available from Penguin in Japan, please write to *Longman Penguin Japan Co Ltd, Yamaguchi Building, 2-12-9 Kanda Jimbocho, Chiyoda-Ku, Tokyo 101, Japan*.